spanish country kitchen

spanish country kitchen

traditional recipes for the home cook

Linda Tubby

photography by Martin Brigdale

RYLAND
PETERS
& SMALL

LONDON NEW YORK

Dedication

For Jennifer and Simon Alvaro Borja Andres Tubby—the Spanish faction of our family—with love.

First published in the USA
by Ryland Peters & Small, Inc.
519 Broadway, 5th Floor
New York, NY 10012
www.rylandpeters.com

10 9 8 7 6 5 4 3 2 1

Library of Congress Cataloging-in-Publication Data

Tubby, Linda.

  Spanish country kitchen : traditional recipes for the home cook / Linda Tubby ; photography by Martin Brigdale.

    p. cm.

  Includes index.

  ISBN 1-84172-946-9

  1. Cookery, Spanish. I. Title.

  TX723.5.S7T83 2005

  641.5946--dc22

                                2005002008

Printed and bound in China

Senior Designer Steve Painter
Commissioning Editor Elsa Petersen-Schepelern
Editor Susan Stuck
Production Patricia Harrington
Art Director Gabriella Le Grazie
Publishing Director Alison Starling

Food Stylist Linda Tubby
Prop Stylist Helen Trent
Indexer Hilary Bird

Notes

• All spoon measurements are level unless otherwise stated.

• All herbs are fresh, unless specified otherwise.

• Eggs are large unless otherwise specified. Uncooked or partly cooked eggs should not be served to the very old, frail, young children, pregnant women, or those with compromised immune systems.

• Most ingredients will be available in larger supermarkets. Others are available in Spanish stores, online, or by mail order (page 142).

Author's Acknowledgements

Without my sister-in-law, this book would not have been possible—a heartfelt thanks for her knowledge and her company during much eating and drinking in Spain and all post requirements so expertly carried out.

A big thanks to Elsa—an editor in a million—so supportive and helpful. For her much "fashing" and all her wordly wisdom.

Special thanks to Steve for such a beautifully designed book and for his support during its creation.

Martin—thank you so much for such great creative and edible photography and lovely scene-setting shots.

Helen for splendidly stylish propping.

Thanks to all who helped at Ryland Peters and Small, especially Gabriella Le Grazie for her enthusiasm and Alison Starling.

My friend Paul Gayler for so much support, endless encouragement and much advice on Spanish cooking.

Señora Maria Esther Montalbo Montero, Juan Ramon Sainz Pardo, and Alicia Nuñez Montalbo for all their kindness and helpful advice in Spain.

Karen and Mike Rogers of Philglas & Swiggot wine merchants, Battersea, London, for their help and advice on Spanish wines and sherry.

Brindisa, especially Claire Roff for all her help and information.

Dan at Mortimer and Bennet for much helpful advice on produce. Phil, Gary, and Eddie at Covent Garden Fish in Chiswick for my usual happy and yummy fish and advice. Andrew at Andreas Georghiou for splendid fresh produce. Rodney at Macken and Collins for meat and service with a smile. Phil at Theobroma for chocolate advice.

Jamie Cañella for advice on all things Spanish.

All family, friends and supporters, who helped in many ways. Jerry for techy help and meals when the candle burnt into the night. With love and thanks to my wonderful, creative sons, Dan and Ben, and my special Mam Lou Simpson, who still amazes me with all her snippets of information.

contents

the spanish country kitchen

Spanish country cooking has its roots in peasant cuisines in which each region relied on seasonal and locally available raw materials. Almost everywhere, traditional cooking is a product of climate and ingredients, history and religion, good times and bad. In Spain, more than anywhere else, cuisine seems to be closely linked to its history and religion.

Wheat, the olive, and the vine go back to Phoenician times, but it was the Romans who made these—together with their beloved garlic—into the staples of Spanish cooking. Soon Spain became one of the agricultural engines of the Empire—as it is today of modern Europe.

The Romans were toppled by the Visigoths, and they, in turn, by the Moors—Muslims from North Africa. It was the Moorish presence that had the greatest and most lasting effect on the Spanish kitchen.

During the time in which they ruled most of Spain, they introduced many foods now thought indigenously Spanish. Oranges and pomegranates, figs and apricots, eggplant and asparagus, almonds and pistachios, sugar and rice, saffron and cinnamon—and the use of nuts and dried fruits in dishes of vegetables, fish, or meat.

The Moors arrived in the 8th century, and stayed for 800 years until defeated in 1492 by Isabella and Ferdinand and expelled from their last great stronghold of Granada.

These same rulers were responsible for two enormous changes in the Spanish kitchen. First, they dispatched Columbus on his voyage of discovery that would win untold gold and other riches from Central and South America. There were culinary riches too, in the form of ingredients such as tomatoes and bell peppers, chiles and chocolate, vanilla and corn, potatoes and beans—all still so much identified with the Spanish cooking of today.

The "Catholic kings," as they were called, were also responsible for the Spanish Inquisition, when the Catholic Church spread its control across the country. The forced conversion or expulsion of the Jews also occurred in 1492, and in 1502 the same fate awaited any Moors who remained. The Spanish culinary emphasis on pork and shellfish—sometimes together—is said to go back to this time. People would ostentatiously consume these dishes in public, because everyone knew that no Jew or Muslim would touch them, therefore the eater must be Christian.

Catholicism also encouraged the Spanish passion for fish. The rule was "fish on Fridays," for the 40 days of Lent, and for innumerable Saints' Days throughout the year. Fresh fish and shellfish came from every coast, even to Madrid in the middle of the country. And if you couldn't have fresh fish, you had *bacalao* (salt cod). Today, salt cod is more expensive than fresh fish, but remains perennially popular.

Though Spaniards do cook at home, city dwellers are social butterflies—snacking at tapas bars and eating out at restaurants and terrazas. In the country however, people necessarily have to cook at home in their own kitchens.

Though modern Spanish kitchens are now like kitchens anywhere, formerly they were like those in other parts of southern Europe. Ovens were the preserve of the village baker, and even when rural houses had brick or stone ovens, they were usually outside. (Understandable when you remember the searing heat of a Spanish summer.)

In many farmhouse kitchens, food was and still is cooked on top of the stove or over a special grill called a *parrillada*, often just outside the kitchen door, because of the heat. Grilled, sautéed, and boiled dishes are the typical home-style recipes. Typically Spanish cooking utensils such as *ollas* (pots), iron paella pans, and terra cotta cazuelas are available outside Spain, but even if you don't have them, ordinary skillets, casseroles, and saucepans will do very well. I hope you enjoy the recipes in this book, as much as I have collecting them.

tapas and salads

tapas, huevos, entradas y ensaladas

Variations of this recipe are found all over Spain. However, I found this version in a tapas bar in a little back street off the Plaza del Sol in Old Madrid. There were mini cazuelas of gambas all lined up, ready to sauté and serve spitting hot to hungry Madrileños during the night's tapas crawl. Serve with a very cold fino sherry.

garlic shrimp
gambas al ajillo

48 small uncooked shrimp, about 1¼ lb., shelled and deveined, with tail shell left on

¼ cup extra virgin olive oil

8 garlic cloves, peeled and bruised

6 small dried chiles

8 small fresh bay leaves

freshly squeezed juice of ½ lemon, plus extra to taste

Alioli

5 garlic cloves, finely chopped

½ cup extra virgin olive oil

½ cup safflower oil

2 teaspoons lemon juice

fine sea salt and freshly ground white pepper

4 individual cazuelas (terra cotta ramekins), 4–5 inches diameter, preheated in a hot oven

Serves 4

To make the alioli, pound the garlic and a large pinch of salt to a smooth, thick, creamy consistency with a mortar and pestle. Slowly drip in ½ cup of the oil, mixing with the pestle. Switch to a whisk and mix in the lemon juice, pepper, and, little by little, another ¼ cup of the oil. Add 1–2 teaspoons cold water and whisk well while adding the remaining oil. The mixture will be very thick. Set aside for at least 30 minutes for the garlic to mellow, then add salt, pepper, and extra lemon juice to taste.

To prepare the shrimp, put on a plate, and sprinkle with a little salt. Heat the oil in a skillet, add the garlic, and sauté until brown. Add the chiles, bay leaves, and shrimp all at once and sauté without turning until the shrimp are crusted and curled on one side, then turn them over and crust the other side, about 3½ minutes in total.

Transfer to the preheated cazuelas, sprinkle with lemon juice, and top with a spoonful of alioli. Serve immediately while still bubbling hot.

Note Alioli, sometimes spelled "allioli," is used with all sorts of dishes. Often an egg yolk is mixed in after the garlic is creamy, making it a little closer to the French aïoli. It's pungent yet delicious. When first made, it is quite strong, but after about 30 minutes the flavor really mellows. For an even milder taste, blanch the garlic cloves until just soft, then pop them out of their skins and pound to a cream.

For information on how to season a terra cotta cazuela, see page 23.

Queso frito is a snack eaten hot, straight from the pan. It is made from Manchego, a sheep's cheese from La Mancha, which is either semi-cured, ripe, or aged with a basket-weave-patterned rind in shades from the palest ocher to deep dark brown and black. Queso frito is one of the most popular tapas, perfect with manzanilla or fino sherry, or with Valdepeñas, a red wine from La Mancha. Sometimes, it is served with membrillo, Spanish quince paste. However, I like it best with a bowl of mixed green and black olives.

fried cheese
queso frito

8–10 oz. semi-cured Manchego cheese, 3 months old

2 tablespoons all-purpose flour

1 egg, beaten

2 cups lightly dried fine fresh white bread crumbs

⅔ cup olive oil

a pinch of smoked sweet paprika (smoked pimentón dulce), to serve

To serve (optional)

membrillo (quince paste)

mixed olives

Serves 6

Cut all the rind from the Manchego and cut the cheese into ½-inch wedges.

Put the flour on a small plate and, working in batches of 6, dip each wedge in the flour, then in the beaten egg, then in the bread crumbs.

Heat half the oil in a nonstick skillet over medium heat, then sauté the wedges in batches until golden—about 45 seconds each side. Drain on paper towels.

Wipe out the pan (to get rid of burnt bread crumbs) and sauté the remaining batches in the same way.

Sprinkle with a pinch of paprika and serve with membrillo or olives, if using.

Note Membrillo is a thick paste made from quinces, a golden fruit related to the apple and pear, available in fall. Quinces are cooked into desserts, jellies, or jams, and into this sweetly smoky paste. Membrillo is also served with a good Manchego cheese instead of dessert.

A tapa is a lid—and the original tapas were slices of bread or small plates put on top of a glass of sherry or wine by the bartender. Soon, delicious foods were used to top the bread or plate, and now we have a huge and delectable range of appetizers served in bars and restaurants from Sydney to Stockholm to Seattle. However, there's nothing to beat the real thing—the best version of this classic I've ever tasted was in a convivial bar in Granada. Serve it very hot, with lots of napkins, toothpicks, a bowl of coarse sea salt, and a copita or two of chilled manzanilla sherry.

potato fritters with chorizo
buñuelos de patatas con chorizo

1 lb. potatoes, peeled and cut lengthwise into thick fingers

1 tablespoon self-rising flour

2 eggs, separated, plus 1 egg white

4 oz. chorizo, skinned and chopped into small pieces

sea salt and freshly ground black pepper

pure olive oil or safflower oil, for deep-frying

Makes about 24

Boil the potatoes in a saucepan of salted water until soft, drain through a colander, and cover with a cloth for about 5 minutes to let them dry out. Transfer to a bowl, mash with the flour, and season with a little pepper. Mix in the egg yolks, then stir in the chorizo.

Put the egg whites in a separate bowl and whisk until soft peaks form. Fold into the mashed potatoes a little at a time.

Fill a saucepan or deep-fryer one-third full with oil, or to the manufacturer's recommended level. Heat to 355°F.

Working in batches of 6, take heaping teaspoons of the mixture and lower into the hot oil. Fry each batch for 3 minutes until evenly golden, turning them over halfway through (if they brown too quickly they will not have a good texture in the center). Keep the oil temperature constant. As each batch is done, drain on paper towels and keep them warm in a preheated oven 350°F until all have been cooked. Serve hot.

Serve on a stick with bowls of olives and pimientos de Padrón, if you can find them in a Spanish store. Emparedados make a great snack served with a glass of draught beer or a good chilled Chardonnay from Penedès.

hot sandwiches
emparedados calientes

8 slices jamón serrano or prosciutto

12 thin slices of sweet chorizo, such as vela dulce from la Rioja

8 slices 3-day-old country bread, crusts removed

2 tablespoons grated Manchego cheese

4 eggs, beaten

½ cup extra virgin olive oil

fine sea salt and freshly ground black pepper

To serve

olives

pimientos de Padrón (optional)

Serves 4: makes 16 pieces

Divide the ham and chorizo between 4 slices of bread, grind over some pepper and sprinkle the grated cheese on top of the chorizo, keeping it to the center of the slices. Put the remaining slices of bread on top and press down firmly.

Put the beaten eggs, salt, and pepper in a flat dish large enough to take 2 sandwiches at a time and dip the sandwiches in the mixture.

Heat half the oil in a nonstick skillet large enough to take 2 sandwiches at a time, then sauté on both sides over medium heat until crisp and golden, 3–3½ minutes each. Repeat with the remaining oil and sandwiches. Cut into triangles, skewer on sticks, and serve while hot with olives, and pimientos de Padrón, if using.

Note Pimientos de Padrón are tiny green peppers named after Padrón in Galicia—you sometimes find them for sale in Spanish shops. They are simply sautéed in olive oil, sprinkled with salt, then you eat them off the stalks, leaving the seeds behind. Be warned—about one in six will be as hot as a chile! Just as you build up confidence, one comes along and blows your head off.

To make them, heat 2 tablespoons virgin olive oil in a large skillet. Working in batches, add 8 oz. fresh green pimientos de Padrón and sauté, shaking the pan, until the skins develop white blisters and the green color intensifies. Remove from the pan, pile onto a plate, and sprinkle with salt.

Migas are a national treasure. They are an ancient and original peasant snack—simply bread sprinkled with salted water, then fried in lovely green olive oil. These are flavored with jamón serrano, but plain ones are served in many ways—sometimes with grapes, or fried eggs, or even with hot chocolate. There are countless regional variations; these are from Extremadura, noted for fine pigs and excellent ham. If serving as a pre-dinner snack, try a Spanish Cava sparkling wine.

migas with jamón
migas de extremadura

8 oz. dry 2-day-old country bread, crusts removed

½ cup extra virgin olive oil

4 oz. jamón serrano or lean slab bacon, cut into ¼ inch pieces,

3 garlic cloves, bruised with the back of a knife

1 fat dried red chile, such as ñora or ancho, seeded and finely chopped

coarse sea salt

Serves 4

Cut the bread into fingers, spread out on a dish towel, then spray or sprinkle lightly with water and a little salt. Wrap up in the towel and leave for 2 hours. Unwrap the cloth and break the bread into big pieces.

Heat 2 teaspoons of the oil in a skillet, add the ham, and sauté until crisp. Drain on paper towels.

Wipe the pan clean and heat the remaining oil. Add the garlic, sauté until golden, then remove and discard. Add all the bread crumbs at once and stir-fry until evenly golden. Stir in the chile and ham and serve very hot. Eat with your fingers or little spoons.

I tasted this as a *pincho* (bar snack) with a few *chatos* (little shots of red wine) in a lovely little bar near the opera house in Madrid—the salt cod with spinach was a taste revelation. When I make this at home, I add some potato as well.

spanish omelet of spinach and salt cod
tortilla de espinacas y bacalao

4 oz. boneless salt cod, cut into cubes

½ cup olive oil

1 small onion, finely chopped

8 oz. potatoes, scrubbed and thinly sliced

6 eggs

4 oz. cooked spinach, from 8 oz. uncooked

freshly ground black pepper

a deep skillet, 8 inches diameter, with rounded sides

Makes 12 pieces

Prepare the salt cod as in the recipe on page 26. Alternatively, make your own salt cod (below). Using your fingers, break up into flakes.

Heat 5 tablespoons of the oil in the skillet, add the onion and potatoes, and sauté for about 10 minutes until soft but not colored—turn them frequently to prevent sticking.

Lightly beat the eggs in a bowl with pepper. It usually isn't necessary to add salt because the fish is already salty. Mix in the spinach and flaked fish.

Pour the mixture into the pan, moving it with a spatula so it flows under and over the potatoes. Cook until set on the bottom—shake the pan as it cooks and loosen the sides a little with a spatula. When it has set and is pale golden, put a plate on top of the pan, turn upside down, then slide the tortilla onto the plate. Put the remaining oil in the pan. When hot, slide the tortilla back into the pan, cooked side up. Cook until golden. Slide onto a board or plate and leave for a minute before slicing.

Note To make your own salt cod, sprinkle a non-reactive dish with 3 tablespoons rock salt and put an 8 oz. skinless cod fillet on top. Cover with another 3 tablespoons salt and chill for 12 hours. Wash off the salt and soak in water for about 2 hours, changing the water several times. This recipe produces an attractive white result—ordinary dried salt cod can be cream in color.

According to Alicia Rios and Lourdes March in their book *The Heritage of Spanish Cooking*, this classic Spanish egg dish was named after the palace of La Flamenca in Aranjuez, the former spring residence of the Spanish kings. Others say it looks like the bright, swirling skirts of a flamenco dancer. Whatever the origin, the result is delicious and easy to make. Serve with fino or manzanilla sherry.

baked eggs with ham and chorizo
huevos a la flamenca

¼ cup olive oil

1 onion, finely chopped

1 garlic clove, crushed

4 oz. cubed Spanish panceta, Italian pancetta, or slab bacon

8 tomatoes, peeled, seeded, and chopped

½ teaspoon sweet paprika (pimentón dulce)

1 tablespoon dry sherry

2 large roasted red bell peppers from a jar or tin, cut into cubes

12 asparagus tips, cooked

½ cup peas, fresh or frozen, blanched

4 very fresh eggs

8 very thin slices of large chorizo, about 1½ oz.

coarse sea salt and freshly ground black pepper

a large cazuela, about 8 inches diameter, or 4 small ones (optional)

Serves 4

Heat the oil in a skillet with an ovenproof handle, add the onion and garlic, and sauté over medium heat for about 7 minutes until soft and just starting to turn golden. Add the panceta and sauté for 3 minutes. Add the tomatoes, paprika, and sherry and cook for about 7 minutes until slightly thickened. Season with a little salt and pepper.

Fold the roasted bell peppers, asparagus, and peas into the mixture. (If finishing in a cazuela, transfer the vegetables to the dish.) Make 4 indentations in the mixture and break in the eggs, swirl the white part slightly, and leave the yolks whole. Bake in a preheated oven at 400°F for about 10 minutes until the eggs have just set.

Meanwhile heat a second small skillet without oil and sauté the chorizo slices on both sides until the oil runs out and the edges are slightly browned. Put on top of the dish and serve.

Note The Spanish method for seasoning a terra cotta cazuela is to submerge it in water for 12 hours, then rub several peeled cloves of garlic over the unglazed base. When the juices have been absorbed into the terra cotta, fill the cazuela with water and ½ cup vinegar and put on top of the stove with a heat-diffusing mat underneath. Bring slowly to a boil and simmer until the liquid has been reduced to about ½ cup. Let cool, rinse with water, and the cazuela is ready to use.

As in all hot countries, cooling salads are a feature of many Spanish meals, in restaurants and in people's homes, served as an appetizer. The most common is either a simple mixture of lettuce and tomato, or the ubiquitous ensalada de San Isidro, which is not unlike a salade Niçoise, with egg, tuna, onion, and olives. This salad comes from Valencia, which gave its name to a variety of sweet orange. A white wine made from the Albariño grape variety will have the zinginess to complement the oranges and enough sweetness to suit the red bell pepper.

orange and potato salad
ensalada valenciana

2 oranges

2 small red onions, cut into slivers

6 medium new potatoes

1 small roasted red bell pepper from a jar, cut into thin strips

fine sea salt and freshly ground green peppercorns

Dressing

1 teaspoon sherry vinegar or red wine vinegar

3 tablespoons safflower oil

2 teaspoons extra virgin olive oil

Serves 4

Remove skin and pith from the oranges and slice the flesh into rounds, keeping any juices for the dressing. Put the slices in a serving dish and add the onions.

To make the dressing, put the collected juice from the oranges in a bowl, add the vinegar, salt, and pepper and gradually whisk in the safflower and olive oils.

Cook the potatoes in a saucepan of boiling salted water. When just soft, drain well, and as soon as they are cool enough, remove the skins and slice the flesh. While still warm, pour over the dressing. When the potatoes are cold, mix into the oranges and onions in the serving dish.

Just before serving, spread the strips of red bell pepper on top, then sprinkle with more crushed green peppercorns.

Note Spanish salads are usually undressed, so the table is set with little containers of salt, oil, and vinegar, so you can dress it yourself. The order is important; first comes plenty of salt, then lots of oil to carry the salt evenly through the leaves or other ingredients and protect them from the vinegar, which is added last and very judiciously.

Xató, pronounced "chay-toh," was originally a fishermen's salad. Salt cod, usually from Norway, was a staple in Catholic Europe, in the Caribbean, and parts of America—interestingly all regions of the world with a plentiful supply of their own fish. It is widely available in Spanish, Italian, Asian, and Caribbean markets, and must be soaked before use to soften it and remove the salt.

The lettuce is traditionally soaked in the sauce for one hour, but I prefer it given less time. This is a simplified version of the sauce found in old cookbooks, but other versions use Romesco Sauce (page 111). Spanish salads usually aren't tossed until you dress them yourself at the table, but this is an exception to the rule. Try to find the great Basque white wine, Txomin Etxanis, with its briny mineral notes—it's excellent with salt cod.

salt cod and tuna salad
xató

8 oz. skinless, boneless salt cod (bacalao), or homemade salt cod (see note page 20)

1 head of escarole lettuce or curly endive, leaves separated and kept in cold water for 30 minutes until crisp

3 slightly green tomatoes, cored and cut into pieces

8 anchovy fillets

8 oz. jar of good-quality tuna in olive oil

12 green olives

12 black olives

Xató sauce

2 dried chiles, about 2 inches long, such as Spanish guindillas

¼ cup red wine vinegar

½ teaspoon salt

10 blanched almonds, lightly toasted in a dry skillet and chopped

3 garlic cloves, finely chopped

½ cup extra virgin olive oil

Serves 6

To prepare the salt cod, soak it in cold water for 12–24 hours, changing the water every 4–5 hours. This softens the flesh and reduces the salt. Just before you are ready to use it, drain well.

To make the sauce, soak the chiles in boiling water for 15 minutes. Drain, seed, and chop coarsely. Put the chiles, vinegar, salt, almonds, and garlic in a blender and pulse to a purée. With the motor running, gradually add the oil. Transfer to a bowl.

Shred the soaked salt cod with your fingers and add to the sauce. Chill for 30 minutes, so the fish "cooks" a little in the acidity of the dressing.

Drain the lettuce and pat dry. Add to the sauce and toss gently. Put the tomatoes, anchovies, and tuna on top of the lettuce, add the olives and toss just before serving.

Cabrales from Asturias and Picón (or Picos de Europa) from Cantabria are outstanding Spanish blue cheeses, with blue veins that are said to be almost purple. They are made from a combination of goats', sheep's and cow's milk from animals grazing on the high pastures of the Picos mountains, in the north of Spain. The whole cheeses are salted, wrapped in leaves, and matured in limestone caves.

Both are excellent served on their own or as part of a cheeseboard with a white wine such as Albariño.

salad of belgian endive and blue cheese
ensalada de endibias al cabrales

8 oz. blue cheese, such as the Spanish Cabrales or Picón, or French Roquefort

⅓ cup light cream

6 heads of Belgian endive or other crisp lettuce

3 tablespoons shelled walnuts, toasted in a dry skillet and roughly broken

¼ teaspoon hot paprika (pimentón picante)

Serves 4

Put three-fourths of the blue cheese in a bowl, then add the cream little by little, mixing to a smooth sauce.

Trim the bases from the endive. Either cut them in half lengthwise or separate the leaves. Add to the bowl of dressing. Sprinkle with the nuts and crumble the remaining cheese over the top. Dust with paprika and serve.

Note Spanish paprika is available in three forms; pimentón dulce is mild and sweet, pimentón picante is spicy hot, and pimentón agridulce is bittersweet. The smoked versions are made from chiles hung whole in traditional mud houses above oak fires that burn for 10–15 days. All are available in gourmet stores or by mail order from sources on page 142.

This is a very fresh, sunny-day sort of salad with clean, crisp flavors. It contains the jewel-like seeds of the pomegranate, a fruit introduced to Spain by the Moors. Their name for it was *granada*, which means "grain," referring to its hundreds of seeds, and they also named their great Andalusian city, Granada, after the pomegranate.

pomegranate salad with frisée leaves
ensalada granadina

1 head of curly endive (frisée)

1 large pomegranate or 2 small

4 oz. young carrots, sliced very finely on a mandoline

3 tablespoons virgin olive oil (see note)

4 garlic cloves, finely sliced

1 tablespoon white wine vinegar

sea salt and freshly ground black pepper

serves 6

To make the endive leaves crisp, separate the leaves, soak in a bowl of cold water for about 30 minutes, then drain and spin in a salad spinner. Break up the leaves into a serving bowl.

Working over a small bowl to catch the juices, open the pomegranate, separate the seeds,and discard the skin and white pith—take care, because the juice stains. Sprinkle the seeds over the lettuce and add the carrot slices.

Put the oil and garlic in a skillet, heat gently, and sauté until just golden. Remove the garlic with a slotted spoon and sprinkle over the leaves.

Add the vinegar to the bowl of pomegranate juices, then whisk in the olive oil from the skillet. Add salt and pepper to taste and let cool for a few minutes. Pour the dressing over the salad and toss just before serving.

Note Extra virgin olive oil would be too strong for the sweet, slightly astringent juices of the pomegranate, so use virgin olive oil instead.

soups and two-course dishes
sopas y cocidas

Spaniards use garlic liberally in their cooking; it is prized for its fine flavor, of course, but also seen as good for the digestion and a cure for all ills. Traditional garlic soup is made with just bread, oil, garlic, and water—healthy, simple food still loved all over Spain. I like to serve it with a poached egg on top, but you might like to try the other common variations listed below. A true, dry, aged amontillado sherry, with its distinctively nutty flavor, would be ideal to drink.

garlic soup with poached egg
sopa de ajo al huevo escalfado

4 slices of bread from a long loaf

6 garlic cloves, lightly crushed but left whole

⅓ cup olive oil

1 teaspoon sweet paprika (pimentón dulce), plus extra for sprinkling

1 teaspoon hot paprika (pimentón picante)

½ teaspoon ground cumin

5 cups clear chicken stock or half stock, half water

4–8 very fresh eggs

sea salt

4 individual ovenproof soup plates or bowls

a baking sheet

Serves 4

Rub the slices of bread with a garlic clove, brush with half the oil, then toast under a preheated moderate broiler until golden. Put into the ovenproof soup plates and set them on the baking sheet.

Heat the rest of the oil in a shallow saucepan, add the garlic, and sauté until golden. Stir in the paprika and cumin, then immediately add the stock and season with salt. Simmer for a few minutes, then pour over the bread. Break 1–2 eggs into the liquid in each plate and transfer to a preheated oven at 400°F until the egg white has set but the yolk is still runny. Alternatively, poach the eggs separately and put on top of the toast, as shown here. Serve immediately, sprinkled with a little paprika.

Variations
• A version of this soup from Castile is made in a cazuela. The eggs are lightly beaten, then poured over the top. The cazuela is put under the broiler and the eggs form a golden surface on the soup.
• In Madrid, they like to serve it with whole eggs broken in, then mixed to cook in the hot broth.

There are more than thirty variations of gazpacho, only some of which are the familiar raw, cold, tomato-based mixture. This version is typical of Andalusia in the hot south. Originally, it was a peasant dish that made use of the three basic ingredients much revered in Spain—oil, water, and bread (in Arabic, *gazpacho* means "soaked bread"). Other ingredients were added according to what was available. If you chill it, put it in a container with a tight-fitting lid so the flavors don't mingle with anything else in the refrigerator.

1 large sweet Spanish onion, finely chopped

1 large red bell pepper, peeled with a vegetable peeler and coarsely chopped

1 large green bell pepper, peeled with a vegetable peeler and coarsely chopped

1½ teaspoons sugar

¼ cup white wine vinegar

3 slices country-style bread, with crusts, about 4 oz.

3 garlic cloves, crushed

5 lb. ripe tomatoes, peeled

5 inches cucumber, peeled and coarsely chopped

⅓ cup virgin olive oil

fine sea salt

a splash of Tabasco (optional)

ice (optional)

Garnishes

2 inches cucumber, unpeeled, finely chopped

½-inch bread croutons, sautéed in olive oil infused with garlic

2 ripe tomatoes, finely chopped

Serves 6

gazpacho

Put one-quarter of the chopped onion in a small bowl and add ¼ teaspoon of the sugar, ½ teaspoon vinegar, and 3 tablespoons cold water and set aside. Reserve one-quarter of the prepared red and green bell peppers and put in small bowls. These small bowls will be served as garnishes at the end.

To make the other garnishes, put the unpeeled chopped cucumber, croutons, and chopped tomatoes in separate small bowls.

To make the gazpacho, put the bread, garlic, and remaining sugar in a flat dish, sprinkle with the remaining vinegar and 1 cup cold water, and let soak.

Cut the peeled tomatoes in half and cut out the hard core. Put a strainer over a bowl and seed the tomatoes into the strainer. Push the seeds with a ladle to extract all the juices. Put the juices in a blender and discard the seeds. Add the soaked bread mixture and half the tomatoes. Blend until smooth and pour into a bowl.

Put the remaining tomatoes, the remaining onion, and ½ cup ice water in the blender. Pulse 8 times to get a medium chunky effect, then pour into the bowl. Put the remaining chopped peppers, coarsely chopped cucumber, oil, salt, and ⅔ cup ice water in the blender and pulse 8 times. Add to the bowl and stir in Tabasco, if using. Chill for up to 2 hours.

If you like ice added, serve with crushed ice cubes. Put the bowls of garnishes on the table for guests to sprinkle over the gazpacho.

White gazpacho is a pale and distinctively interesting version that certainly predates the tomato recipe. The Moors brought almonds to Spain about seven centuries before the arrival of tomatoes and bell peppers from the New World. The grapes are usually peeled, but if time is short just squash them a little to release their flavor. The gazpacho is generally served very cold, but cold grapes lose their flavor, so add them just before serving. Serve with a well-aged amontillado sherry.

chilled almond soup with grapes
gazpacho blanco con uvas

⅔ cup blanched almonds

2 garlic cloves, crushed

3 slices of bread, crusts removed

3 tablespoons white wine vinegar

1 teaspoon salt

a scant ½ cup extra virgin olive oil

To serve

about 1 cup (6 oz.) assorted green and black grapes, peeled and pitted

¼ cup extra virgin olive oil

Serves 4

Grind the almonds as finely as possible in an electric coffee grinder and put in a blender with the garlic, bread, vinegar, and salt. Add 1 cup cold water, work to a purée, then, using the back of a ladle, push through a strainer set over a bowl.

Put the solids back in the blender with about 1½ cups extra cold water, depending on the thickness required. With the motor running, gradually add the oil. Chill in the refrigerator for up to 2 hours.

Pour into 4 chilled soup bowls, add the grapes, and drizzle 1 tablespoon extra virgin olive oil over each serving.

Note Serve as a appetizer, or in small glasses for a picnic or a party.

Aranjuez, just south of Madrid, is famous for its royal palace, its beautiful gardens, strawberries, and asparagus. In April, the street stalls are piled high with huge bundles of fat and thin, wonderfully bright green asparagus as well as the fat white variety so popular in mainland Europe. Soups go well with sherry—try a manzanilla with this dish.

cream of asparagus soup
crema de espárragos

1½ lb. asparagus
3 tablespoons olive oil
1 tablespoon butter
2 leeks, well washed and thinly sliced
1 onion, finely chopped
1 quart chicken stock
freshly grated nutmeg
⅔ cup heavy cream
sea salt and freshly ground white pepper

Serves 4

Cut the tips off 8 asparagus spears and reserve. Chop the rest into ¾-inch pieces.

Heat the oil and butter in a saucepan, add the leeks and onion, cover, and sauté over gentle heat for 10 minutes. Add the chopped asparagus, stock, and a grinding of nutmeg, season well with salt and pepper, and simmer for 10 minutes.

Transfer to a blender, purée until smooth, then, using the back of a ladle, push through a strainer set over a bowl. Alternatively, use a mouli. Add two-thirds of the cream to the bowl and stir well. Return the soup to the saucepan and heat gently when ready to serve (do not let boil).

Cook the reserved asparagus tips in boiling water until just tender. Ladle the soup into bowls, spoon the remaining cream on top, add the asparagus tips and another grinding of nutmeg, then serve.

In all traditional Spanish recipes, there are many variations on a theme; this is no exception. Often the soup has just bread to thicken the liquid, but this version uses *fideos* (or Spanish noodles). I have used a mixture of pork and veal to make the meatballs, but it would be fine to use just pork.

Try a typical red wine from Catalonia, such as Priorat—dark, almost inky black. Alternatively, seek out wines from neighboring Montsant, made with the Spanish version of the French Grenache grape, Garnacha.

5 cups chicken stock

2 tablespoons tomato purée

4 tomatoes, peeled, seeded, and finely chopped

⅓ cup fideos (see note)

sea salt and freshly ground white pepper

mint leaves, to serve

meatballs

6 oz. ground pork

6 oz. ground veal

1 small onion, grated

1 garlic clove, crushed

1 egg, beaten

1 tablespoon chopped fresh mint

2 tablespoons chopped fresh parsley

1 tablespoon fine freshly made bread crumbs

a pinch of cinnamon

sea salt and freshly ground black pepper

all-purpose flour, for dusting

2 tablespoons olive oil, for cooking

Serves 4–6

catalan meatball soup
sopa de albóndiguillas catalana

To make the meatballs, put the ground pork and veal in a bowl with the grated onion, garlic, egg, chopped mint, and half the chopped parsley. Stir in the bread crumbs, cinnamon, salt, and pepper. Using your hands, mix to a paste and form into ½-inch balls. Toss in flour until lightly coated.

Heat the oil in a skillet and sauté the balls over high heat to give a little color and to firm them up a little.

To make the soup, put the stock in a large saucepan and bring to a boil. Add the tomato purée, tomatoes, fideos noodles, salt, and pepper.

Add the meatballs to the pan and simmer gently for 5 minutes. Stir in the remaining parsley and serve with the mint leaves on top.

Note In Catalonia, the regional name for *fideos* is *fideus*. If you can't find this Spanish pasta, buy the broken vermicelli sold in the kosher section of supermarkets or at Jewish delis for making chicken soup.

This meal-in-a-pot forms the classic family feast beloved of all Spaniards, rich or poor, in every region. It is known by different names in each area, but is essentially the same dish. It comes in two parts; first you eat the broth with the noodles, then the meat and sausages, with the vegetables and chickpeas. Set the table with large soup bowls at each place.

el cocido

1¼ cups dried chickpeas

2 teaspoons salt, plus extra for the cabbage

1½ lb. beef brisket, rolled

1 lb. piece of belly pork or other fat pork, without skin and bones

1 lb. smoked bacon, unsliced

2 whole chicken legs

2 fresh bay leaves

2 small onions

6 small carrots

a bunch of small turnips

a bunch of flat-leaf parsley, tied together

2 sweet chorizos (chorizo dulce)

2 morcilla, Spanish salchicha, or Italian or French-style fresh pork sausages (optional)

1 lb. new potatoes

1 small Savoy cabbage

2 tablespoons extra virgin olive oil

2 garlic cloves, bashed until bruised and split

1 cup fideos or fine vermicelli noodles

pickled mild green chiles, to serve

a large piece of cheesecloth

Serves 6-8

The day before you want to serve the cocido, put the chickpeas in a bowl and cover well with cold water, mix in 2 teaspoons salt, and leave overnight.

Also the day before, put the beef, belly pork, bacon, chicken legs, and bay leaves in a large saucepan or stockpot. Add cold water to cover by 1 inch. Bring slowly to a boil and simmer gently for 45 minutes. Remove the chicken legs, put them in a bowl, cool, cover, and chill. Continue cooking the other meats for 30 minutes. Transfer to a bowl, let cool, cover, then chill. The next day, skim the fat off the meat.

Drain the chickpeas and put in a saucepan with cold water to cover by ¾ inch, bring to a rapid boil, and when the froth rises, add a cup of cold water and skim. Repeat once more, then simmer for 15 minutes. Drain the chickpeas through a colander lined with cheesecloth. Put one of the onions on top, then tie up the cheesecloth into a bag.

Put the bag of chickpeas in a large stockpot, then add the cooked beef, pork, and bacon, the other onion, carrots, turnips, parsley, and skimmed stock. Slowly bring to a very gentle simmer, then continue simmering for 30 minutes.

Meanwhile, bring a second saucepan of water to a boil and blanch the chorizos and morcilla or pork sausages for 5 minutes over low heat. Drain and add to the meats. Add the potatoes to the meats and cook everything on very low heat for a further 30–45 minutes. Add the chicken for the last 20 minutes. Check to make sure everything is tender.

Cut the cabbage into 1-inch pieces, cook in a saucepan of boiling salted water for 5 minutes, then drain. Heat the oil in a skillet and sauté the garlic until just golden, then remove the garlic, add the cabbage, and sauté for 2 minutes.

Remove 5 cups of stock from the meats, transfer to a saucepan, add the fideos, bring to the boil, cook for 5 minutes, then transfer to a tureen to serve.

Cut up the meats and sausages and put them on a serving platter. Take the meat off the chicken and add to the platter. Add the turnips and carrots. Put the chickpeas on a second plate and add the cabbage. Put everything on the table and let everyone help themselves.

rice, pasta, and savory pies
arroz, pastas y masa

A two-course dish of rice and fish. The rice is cooked in a rich stock, then the fish and shellfish are eaten with pungently flavored salsas (or you can just eat them together). In Valencia and Alicante, this is just as popular as the better-known seafood paella.

rice "apart" with seafood
arroz abanda

1½ lb. halibut fillets

12 medium unshelled shrimp

4 langoustines or extra shrimp

1 lb. clams

3 tablespoons olive oil

1 medium onion, finely chopped

2 garlic cloves, finely chopped

5 tomatoes, peeled, seeded, and finely chopped

1½ cups Spanish rice, such as bomba or paella rice

sea salt and freshly ground black pepper

Stock

1 tablespoon olive oil

1 medium onion, finely chopped

1 garlic clove, finely chopped

2 tomatoes, coarsely chopped

2–3 fish frames and 1 fish head (from the fish seller)

a pinch of saffron threads, toasted in a dry skillet, then crushed

3 bay leaves

3 sprigs of parsley

sea salt and freshly ground black pepper

To serve

Salsa Salmoretta (page 91) or Salsa Romesco (page 111)

Alioli (page 11)

a paella pan

kitchen foil

Serves 4

To prepare the fish and seafood, cut the halibut into 2-inch pieces and season lightly with salt and pepper. Shell and devein the shrimp, leaving the tail fins on. Reserve the shells.

Put 1¾ cups cold water in a saucepan and bring to a boil. Add a pinch of salt and cook the shrimp and langoustines for 2 minutes. Remove with a slotted spoon and transfer to a bowl. Return the water to a boil, add the clams, cover, and cook for 1½ minutes until they open. Strain through a colander over a bowl, reserving the liquid. Rinse the clams briefly under the cold tap to stop them cooking, then add to the shrimp and langoustines.

To make the stock, heat the 1 tablespoon oil in a saucepan, add the onion and garlic, and sauté until softened. Add the 2 tomatoes, then cook for 3 minutes over medium heat. Add the fish bones and head, shrimp shells, saffron, bay leaves, parsley, salt, pepper, and 3 cups cold water. Slowly bring to a boil, lower the heat, and simmer for 25 minutes. Strain through a fine-meshed sieve.

Meanwhile, heat a paella pan or a large skillet with ovenproof handle, add the 3 tablespoons oil, onion, and garlic. Sauté until golden. Add the 5 tomatoes and cook until they soften to a sauce. Stir in the rice and 2 cups of the stock. Season with salt and pepper and simmer for 3 minutes. Transfer to a preheated oven and cook at 400°F for 10 minutes. Add 1 cup of the clam liquid and cook for a further 5 minutes. Remove from the oven and keep warm.

Put the remaining clam liquid and remaining fish stock in an ovenproof dish, add the halibut, cover, and cook in the oven for 5 minutes. Turn the oven off. Add the seafood to the halibut and cover with foil. Loosely cover the rice with foil and put both foil-covered dishes back in the oven for a further 5 minutes. Transfer the rice to a serving dish and the fish and seafood to a separate platter.

Serve the rice first, followed by the seafood with salsa salmoretta or romesco and alioli.

1/4 cup olive oil

3 chicken breasts with skin, cut into 4 pieces each

2 skinless duck breasts, cut into 5 pieces each

1 red bell pepper, seeded and cut into long chunks

2 small hot chorizos (picante), skin removed, flesh cut into 1/2-inch slices

2 tomatoes, peeled, seeded, and chopped

1 teaspoon sweet paprika (pimentón dulce)

a large pinch of saffron

2 sprigs of rosemary

1 quart clear chicken stock or water

4 oz. thin green beans

1 cup shelled fava beans (optional), (from 1 lb. before podding)

1/2 cup cooked white Spanish beans (alubias), butter beans or haricots

1 cup shelled peas

1 1/3 cups bomba or other short grain paella rice (do not wash)

coarse sea salt

1 onion, cut into wedges, soaked in cold water for 5 minutes, to serve

a paella pan

Serves 4–6

The Albufera in the Valencia region is a large lagoon where the Moors planted rice in the 8th century. The fertile land beyond, known as *huertas* (gardens), offered all the goodies necessary to make this original paella. People used what was available from the land, not the sea (that version came later), such as rabbit, duck, snails, eels, vegetables, herbs, and rice.

The pan is crucial to the success of paella: it should be wide and shallow with two handles, ideal for the traditional method of cooking over an open fire. Cooked this way, a golden crust forms on the bottom and sides: this is called *socarrat* and is much prized.

Serve with an Albariño or an oaky Chardonnay.

traditional chicken paella
paella valenciana de la huerta

Heat the oil in a paella pan set over 2 burners or over a preheated outdoor grill. Add the chicken and duck and sauté on all sides until golden. Halfway through cooking, add the red pepper and chorizos. Add the tomatoes, paprika, saffron, rosemary, and salt, then pour in all the stock. Bring to a boil, then lower the flame so it simmers very gently for 15 minutes.

Add the green and white beans and the peas. Pour in the rice (traditionally in the form of a cross). Mix into the stock—do not stir again. Let cook over low heat for another 15 minutes.

Increase the heat to high for 1 minute—this creates the socarrat if you aren't cooking the paella over an open fire.

Remove from the heat and leave for 5–10 minutes before serving with raw onion wedges. (It is important to serve it warm, not hot.)

This vegetarian dish comes from Valencia, where it is served during the Lenten fast. Its Spanish name means "with partridge"—though the partridge is really a whole bulb of garlic. I like to use bomba rice, especially a brand called La Perdiz, with a drawing of a little partridge on its smart cloth sack. It is also good for soups, because the grains stay firm. Another wonderful variety is Calasparra rice from Murcia, just south of Valencia. Sold in numbered cotton bags, it is the best Spanish rice available. This kind of rice absorbs liquid without turning sticky, but there are rules— never wash it and stir it only once. Bomba will absorb double its own volume of liquid and the Calasparra up to three or four times.

baked rice with garlic
arroz al horno con perdiz

1½ cup olive oil

1 whole head of garlic

1 large onion, finely chopped

4 tomatoes, peeled, seeded, and chopped (keep the juices)

1 teaspoon sweet paprika (pimentón dulce)

2 cups Spanish rice, such as bomba

up to 1 quart vegetable stock or water

2 cups canned chickpeas, 15 oz., rinsed and drained

⅓ cup raisins, soaked in hot water for 30 minutes until plump

sea salt and freshly ground black pepper

a paella pan, cazuela, or other ovenproof pan, 8–10 inches diameter

aluminum foil

Serves 6

Heat the oil in a paella pan, heatproof cazuela, heatproof shallow casserole dish, or a skillet with ovenproof handle. Add the garlic head and onion and sauté for 12 minutes over low heat until the garlic is pale golden and beginning to soften and the onion soft and golden.

Remove the garlic and reserve. Increase the heat and add the tomatoes and juices. Cook until the mixture starts to thicken a little. Stir in the paprika, salt and pepper.

Stir in the rice. Add half the stock or water and bring slowly to a boil. Add the chickpeas, drain the raisins, and gently fold them into the rice. Put the garlic in the center and bake in a preheated oven at 350°F for 10 minutes. Heat the remaining stock or water, then add as much as the rice seems to need. Continue baking for 10–15 minutes before serving, covering the top with foil if it seems to be over-browning or drying out. Serve from the pan.

The Moors introduced pasta to Catalonia in the form of *fideus* or *fideos*—short, thin pasta pieces, like Jewish vermicelli. The cooking methods for this dish bring together the two cornerstones of Catalan cooking. The first, *sofregit*, called *sofrito* elsewhere in Spain, is the basis for many dishes and sauces. In essence, it is lightly sautéed garlic and onions, with tomatoes and various other additions. The second is *picada*, a crushed mixture of fried bread, garlic, nuts, and herbs, moistened and used as flavoring and a thickener.

¼ cup olive oil

12 oz. spareribs, chopped into 2-inch pieces, then sprinkled with salt

8 oz. fresh spicy pork sausages (not chorizo), cut into 1-inch lengths

8 oz. fideos pasta or Jewish vermicelli (page 43)

2¾ cups chicken stock, preferably homemade

sea salt and freshly ground black pepper

Sofregit (sofrito)

4 tablespoons olive oil

2 medium onions, finely chopped

1 garlic clove, finely chopped

4 tomatoes, peeled, seeded and chopped

½ teaspoon sweet paprika (pimentón dulce)

Picada

1 thick slice of country bread, fried in olive oil

1 garlic clove, chopped

½ cup pine nuts, lightly toasted in a dry skillet

3 tablespoons finely chopped flat-leaf parsley

a paella pan or other shallow ovenproof pan, 8–10 inches diameter

Serves 4

catalan pasta
fideus a la catalana

Heat 1 tablespoon of the oil in a paella pan, shallow heatproof casserole dish, or skillet with ovenproof handle. Add the spareribs and sausage, sauté for 3 minutes on each side, then transfer to a plate. Wipe the pan clean and heat the remaining 3 tablespoons of the oil, add the pasta, and sauté over high heat for about 4 minutes until evenly golden. Transfer to a bowl.

To make the sofregit, heat the ¼ cup oil in the same pan, add the onions and garlic, and sauté for 5 minutes over low heat. Increase the heat, add the tomatoes, then cook for about 3 minutes until thickened. Stir in the paprika.

Add the ribs and sausages, and push them down into the tomatoes, add the stock, salt, and pepper, and bring to a boil. Fold in the crisp pasta.

Bake in a preheated oven at 375°F for 5 minutes. Stir in 1¾ cups boiling water and return to the oven for another 5 minutes. Push the crisp noodles from the top under the liquid and bake for another 10 minutes.

Meanwhile, to make the picada, cut the fried bread into pieces and put in a small processor with the garlic, pine nuts, and parsley. Pulse to form a paste. Loosen with about ¼ cup boiling water, then fold into the pan of pasta.

Set the pan under a preheated broiler about 8 inches from the heat for about 5 minutes just to crisp the top a little (don't let it burn). Serve from the pan.

fish and seafood

pescados y mariscos

A classic dish from Santiago de Compostella, inland from the Atlantic coast of Galicia, where scallops grow in abundance. Santiago (St. James) is the patron saint of Spain and the scallop shell is his emblem. For over a thousand years, pilgrims have made the long, arduous journey to this shrine, and in former times used scallop shells to scoop water from the streams. Today, the town is festooned with strings of shells painted with the sword of St. James (page 137). The French scallop dish, Coquilles St. Jacques, is named after the same saint. If you don't have scallop shells for this recipe, use small gratin dishes.

baked scallops
vieiras al gallego

6 large scallops

¼ cup extra virgin olive oil

1 medium onion, very finely chopped

1 garlic clove, finely chopped

1 medium-hot dried chile, such as guindilla, seeded and finely crushed

½ teaspoon sweet paprika (pimentón dulce)

8 oz. tomatoes, seeded and finely chopped

1 tablespoon brandy

½ cup fine fresh bread crumbs

2 tablespoons finely chopped fresh flat-leaf parsley

sea salt

4 large scallop shells or small gratin dishes

Serves 4

Cut the scallops in half horizontally and arrange 3 halves in each scallop shell or gratin dish. Season lightly.

Heat 2 tablespoons of the oil in a skillet, add the onion and garlic, and sauté until very soft but not colored. Stir in the chile, paprika, and tomatoes and cook for 3 minutes over medium heat. Add the brandy and continue cooking until thickened.

Mix the bread crumbs with the parsley and a little salt. Spoon an equal amount of sauce over each scallop dish and sprinkle with the bread crumb mixture. Spoon over the remaining oil and bake under a medium-hot broiler for 5 minutes until golden. Serve at once.

Note One of the leading white wine varieties of Spain is Albariño, a favorite in trendy tapas bars from Barcelona to Madrid. It comes from the Rías Baixas region on the Atlantic coast between Santiago and the Portuguese border. Excellent, dry, and aromatic, it is a great partner for all kinds of seafood.

I use small squid for this recipe. Even smaller ones, calamaritos, are only 1 inch long and are delicious fried in a light batter to serve as a tapa. Calamares are also cooked *en su tinta* (in their own ink)—black, shiny, and very good—and as *fritos a la romana* (floured and fried squid rings). All are popular as tapas too.

stuffed calamares
calamares rellenos

⅓ cup extra virgin olive oil

1 medium onion, finely chopped

16 ready prepared baby squid with tentacles, about 3 inches long (see note)

2 oz. chorizo, finely chopped

½ teaspoon chile flakes

2 garlic cloves, finely chopped

½ cup pine nuts

¾ cup fresh bread crumbs

2 tablespoons finely chopped fresh flat-leaf parsley, plus extra coarsely chopped, to serve

Tomato sauce

2 tablespoons extra virgin olive oil

1 onion, finely chopped

1 garlic clove, finely chopped

½ teaspoon sugar

6 medium tomatoes, peeled, seeded, and finely chopped (retain any juices)

Serves 4

Heat 3 tablespoons of the oil in a skillet, add the onion, and sauté until soft and pale golden. Add the chopped tentacles and sauté until pale. Add the chorizo and sauté until the fat runs out into the onion. Stir in the chile flakes.

Toast the pine nuts in a dry skillet for a minute or so until golden. Take care, because they will burn easily. Transfer to a plate to cool.

Meanwhile, put the garlic, half the pine nuts, and bread crumbs in a processor and pulse until fine. Add to the pan, stir in the parsley, and let cool.

To make the tomato sauce, heat the oil in a flameproof casserole dish, add the onion and garlic, and sauté until pale gold. Increase the heat, add the sugar and the tomatoes with their juice, then simmer for a few minutes.

Stuff the squid with the cold mixture and close with a toothpick. Heat the oil in a skillet and sauté the stuffed squid on both sides until pale golden, about 2 minutes on each side. Add to the casserole dish and cook in a preheated oven at 375°F for 15 minutes. Remove from the oven, sprinkle with parsley and remaining toasted pine nuts and serve.

Note If you have to clean the squid yourself, first pull off the tentacles. Rinse out the bodies and discard the stiff transparent quill if any. Cut the tentacles away from the head and discard the head. Chop the tentacles into small pieces.

Zarzuela is from the Catalan word for light opera or variety show—a medley in fact—and this medley is a feast in a pan. Add any fish or shellfish you like, as long as it's firm enough not to flake into shreds—use whatever is available on the day.

12 mussels

12 clams

1 cup dry white wine

8 oz. monkfish fillet, skinned and cut into large chunks

8 oz. halibut fillet, cut into large chunks

6 large peeled shrimp, tail fins on

⅓ cup virgin olive oil

6 cooked langoustines or extra shrimp

sea salt and freshly ground black pepper

2 lemons, cut into wedges, to serve

Picada

2 slices fried white bread, cut into cubes

2 garlic cloves, coarsely chopped

9 almonds, coarsely chopped

½ cup extra virgin olive oil

Sofregit

2 tablespoons olive oil

1 onion, finely chopped

1 garlic clove, crushed

2 teaspoons sweet paprika (pimentón dulce)

1 cup (8 oz.) canned chopped tomatoes

½ teaspoon saffron threads, soaked in 1 tablespoon boiling water

3 bay leaves

sea salt and freshly ground black pepper

Serves 4

zarzuela
zarzuela de mariscos

To make the picada, put the fried bread in a small processor with the garlic and almonds and blend finely. With the motor running, gradually add the oil to form a loose paste.

To prepare the mussels and clams, put the wine in a large saucepan and bring to a boil. Add the mussels and clams, cover, and cook over medium heat for about 2 minutes—shake the pan after 1 minute—until all the shells have opened. (Discard any that haven't.) Pour into a colander set over a bowl to catch all the liquid. Transfer the mussels and clams to a bowl and cover loosely. Reserve the liquid to use in the sofregit.

To make the sofregit, heat the oil in a saucepan, add the onion and garlic, and sauté gently until pale golden and soft. Stir in the paprika, tomatoes, and saffron and its soaking water. Pour the mussel liquid carefully through a fine-meshed strainer, leaving any sediment behind. Add the bay leaves, salt, and pepper. Cover and cook over medium heat for 10 minutes. Add a little water if the mixture gets too thick.

Season the monkfish, halibut, and shrimp with salt and pepper. Heat 2 tablespoons of the oil in a skillet, add the pieces of monkfish and halibut, and sauté until lightly golden on both sides. Remove to a plate and keep them warm. Deglaze the pan with 3 tablespoons water and pour into the simmering sofregit.

Wipe the skillet, add the remaining 3 tablespoons oil and the shrimp, and sauté just until they turn pink on both sides. Add the langoustines to heat through for 1 minute, turning frequently. Pour in the cooked sofregit and add the rest of the seafood, including the mussels and clams. Heat very gently for a few minutes to ensure everything is cooked through. Loosen the picada with a little liquid from the pan and fold into the seafood. Serve with the lemon wedges.

A mixture of very finely chopped vegetables forms the basis of this dish. In can be served either very hot straight from the oven or left until cold, which I like in summer. In winter, you could use fresh herrings instead. In true Spanish style, eat it with bread to mop up the juices—no Spaniard would ever sit down to a meal without lots of good bread.

baked sardines
sardinas en cazuela

⅓ cup extra virgin olive oil

1 red bell pepper, seeded and finely chopped

2 medium onions, very finely chopped

3 garlic cloves, crushed

2 large tomatoes, peeled, seeded, and cut into 1-inch cubes

1 teaspoon hot paprika (pimentón picante)

a pinch of saffron

¼ teaspoon ground cumin

2 bay leaves

2 tablespoons chopped fresh flat-leaf parsley, plus extra leaves to serve

9–12 fresh sardine fillets (depending on the size of the dish)

sea salt and freshly ground black pepper

a medium cazuela or ovenproof dish

Serves 4–6

Heat 3 tablespoons of the oil in a skillet, add the bell pepper, onions, and garlic, and cook gently until softened but not colored, 8–10 minutes. Add the tomatoes, paprika, saffron, cumin, and bay leaves and cook for a further 5–8 minutes (add a little water if the mixture sticks to the pan) until completely cooked. Season with salt and pepper and fold in the parsley.

Put the sardine fillets on a tray skin side down and sprinkle with a little salt and pepper.

Arrange one-third of the fillets skin side up in the cazuela or ovenproof dish, then cover with one-third of the cooked mixture. Repeat twice more—when adding the last layer, let the silver sardine skin peek through. Grind over a little more pepper and spoon over the rest of the oil.

Bake the cazuela in a preheated oven at 375°F for 15–20 minutes until sizzling. Sprinkle with the whole parsley leaves, then serve.

Orense is on the river Miño in Galicia, a region of fabulous fish and passionate fish lovers. Although most of us have to be content with farmed fish, this area is famous for its trout-fishing streams. There is a Spanish saying that trout is never better than when *fresca frita y fría*—in other words "fresh, fried, and cold." This recipe is testament to this, except it is also wonderful served hot. Excellent with the local white wine variety, Albariño—fruity yet delicate.

fresh fried trout
truchas fritas a la orensana

3 tablespoons olive oil

4 oz. cubed Spanish panceta, Italian pancetta, slab bacon, or ham

2 trout, cleaned

2 tablespoons all-purpose flour, seasoned with salt and pepper

1 garlic clove, cut into slivers

2 tablespoons chopped fresh flat-leaf parsley

sea salt and freshly ground black pepper

1 lemon, cut into wedges, to serve

Serves 2

Heat 1 tablespoon of the oil in a skillet, add the panceta, and sauté until just golden. Remove to a plate.

Dust the fish with the seasoned flour. Open the bellies, season with salt and pepper, and put in the garlic slivers.

Heat the remaining oil in the skillet, add the trout, and sauté over medium heat for 3 minutes on each side. Increase the heat and cook for a further 2 minutes on each side. Transfer to hot plates, then return the panceta to the pan to warm through. Spoon the panceta on top of the trout and sprinkle with parsley and pepper. Serve hot with lemon wedges, or leave until cold.

Note *Panceta* is Spanish bacon, like Italian pancetta. *Panceta ahumada* is smoked streaky bacon. Both are available cut from slabs in Spanish stores.

Sea bass has the perfect texture for this dish, which is my favorite fish recipe. Serve with lots of bread and enjoy a nice crisp wine made from the Parellada grape, perfect for a summer lunch under a vine-laden awning. I use virgin olive oil, not extra virgin: extra virgin is too powerful for the mildly acidic flavors of this dish.

sea bass in vinaigrette with capers and parsley
lubina en vinagreta con alcaparras

2 cups dry white wine

zest from 1 unwaxed lemon, peeled off in wide strips

zest from 1 unwaxed orange, peeled off in wide strips

3–4 large shallots or red onions, finely sliced

a handful of parsley stalks

2 lb. sea bass fillets (4–8, depending on size)

2 tablespoons white wine vinegar

½ teaspoon sugar

⅓ cup virgin olive oil

3 tablespoons capers, drained and rinsed

3 tablespoons fresh flat-leaf parsley leaves

sea salt and freshly ground black pepper

Serves 4

Working in 2 batches, put 1 cup of the wine and 1 cup cold water in a shallow pan such as a non-stick skillet. Add half the strips of lemon and orange zest, 1 of the shallots, half the parsley stalks, and salt. Add half the sea bass fillets and slowly bring to a gentle simmer, about 5 minutes. As soon as the liquid starts to bubble, take the pan off the heat and leave for 2 minutes. Transfer the fillets to a serving dish and keep them warm, while you repeat with the second batch, using 1 cup wine, 1 cup cold water, the remaining strips of zest, 1 shallot, the remaining parsley, and some salt.

Meanwhile, soak the remaining shallot in the vinegar for about 3 minutes. Drain off the vinegar into a bowl and use to make the dressing. Reserve the soaked shallot.

Add the sugar, salt, and pepper to the vinegar and whisk in the olive oil, a little at a time. Mix in the shallot or onion, capers, and parsley and pour over the fish fillets while they are still hot. Let cool and eat after 1–2 hours.

Marmitako is from the Basque region and the name comes from the French word *marmite*—a tall, straight-sided stewpot made from copper, iron, or earthenware. The fishermen used to make this stew on board their boats, using bonito or albacore tuna from the Bay of Biscay, mopping up the soupy juices with lots of delicious fried bread. Try one of the crisp, grapey, thirst-quenching white wines from the Basque region, such as Chacoli de Getaria and Chacoli de Bizkaia.

tuna and potato stew
marmitako

1 small red bell pepper

1 small yellow bell pepper

1 small green bell pepper

3 tablespoons extra virgin olive oil

1 large onion, finely chopped

2 garlic cloves, finely chopped

5 tomatoes, peeled, seeded, and chopped (reserve any juices)

½ teaspoon sweet paprika (pimentón dulce)

1 bay leaf

1 lb. potatoes, peeled and cut into ½-inch slices

2 slices of fresh tuna, 1 lb. each, each cut into 6 chunky pieces

2 tablespoons parsley leaves, torn

sea salt and freshly ground black pepper

Fried bread

6 slices of white bread, cut into triangles

extra virgin olive oil, for sautéing

Serves 4–6

Halve and seed the red, yellow, and green bell peppers and cut the flesh into ½-inch cubes.

Heat the oil in a heatproof casserole dish, add the onion, garlic, and peppers, and sauté over low heat until softened but not colored, 12–15 minutes. Increase the heat and stir in the tomatoes and their juice. When the mixture starts to thicken, add the paprika, bay leaf, salt, and pepper.

Stir in the potatoes and 1¾ cups boiling water and simmer gently for about 15 minutes until the potatoes are cooked.

Meanwhile, to make the fried bread, heat the olive oil in a large skillet, add the triangles of bread, and sauté on both sides until golden. Remove and drain on paper towels.

Season the pieces of tuna 10 minutes before use. Add the tuna to the casserole dish and after about 30 seconds, when the underside turns pale, turn the pieces over and turn off the heat. Leave for 5 minutes. Sprinkle with parsley and serve with the triangles of fried bread.

Spaniards insist on the freshest of fish. Even in Madrid, in the middle of Spain, the catch is rushed from every coast to reach markets and restaurants in superb condition. This recipe is a good dish for a large family. If red bream isn't available, use red snapper.

baked red bream
besugo al horno

2 lb. red bream or red snapper fillets, cut into 2½-inch pieces

½ lemon, cut into thin wedges

3 tablespoons fine fresh bread crumbs

2 garlic cloves, crushed

2 tablespoons hot paprika (pimentón picante)

1 tablespoon finely chopped flat-leaf parsley

4 medium potatoes, thinly sliced

7 tablespoons extra virgin olive oil

12 black olives, such as aragón

sea salt and freshly ground black pepper

an oiled ovenproof dish large enough to hold the fish in a single layer

Serves 4

Make a slash on the skin of each piece of fish, then lightly salt all over, then insert a lemon wedge into each slash.

Mix the bread crumbs, garlic, paprika, and parsley in a bowl.

Put a layer of the potatoes in the oiled ovenproof dish. Sprinkle the potatoes with salt and pepper, then spoon over 2 tablespoons of oil and ¼ cup water. Bake in a preheated oven at 375°F for 30–40 minutes.

Put the fish on top, sprinkle with the breadcrumb mixture, and pour the remaining olive oil over the top. Pour 2 more tablespoons of water around the sides of the dish (so the crumbs don't get wet) and bake for a further 10 minutes.

Dot with the olives, cover the dish, and cook for a further 5–10 minutes until the potatoes are soft and the fish flakes easily.

The traditional cooking pan for this dish is the cazuela—a wide, flat, terra cotta casserole dish, glazed except for the base. It has amazing heat-retaining properties and is excellent for dishes that rely on slow, even heat. If cooking on top of the stove, use a heat-diffusing mat.

hake in garlic sauce with clams
merluza al pil-pil con almejas

1 lb. clams

½ cup dry white wine

6 hake or cod steaks, cut 1 inch thick through the bone

⅔ cup olive oil

4 garlic cloves, thinly slivered

¼ cup chopped fresh flat-leaf parsley

sea salt and freshly ground black pepper

a cazuela or heavy skillet

cheesecloth

Serves 4–6

Put the clams and wine in a saucepan over high heat. As they open, remove them to a bowl and cover with plastic wrap. Discard any that fail to open. Pour the cooking juices through a cheesecloth-lined strainer and set aside.

Put the fish on a plate and sprinkle with salt 10 minutes before cooking.

Put the oil and garlic in a cazuela or heavy skillet and heat gently so the garlic turns golden slowly and doesn't burn. Remove the garlic with a slotted spoon and keep until ready to serve.

Pour about two-thirds of the oil into a pitcher and add the fish to the oil left in the pan. Cook over very low heat, moving the pan in a circular motion—keep taking it off the heat so it doesn't cook too quickly (the idea is to encourage the oozing of the juices instead of letting them sauté and burn). Add the remaining oil little by little as you move the pan, so an emulsion starts to form. When all the oil has been added, remove the fish to a plate and keep it warm. Put the pan back on the heat, add the reserved clam juices, and stir to form a creamy sauce.

Return the fish to the pan, add the chopped parsley, and continue to cook until the fish is tender, about 5 minutes. Just before serving, add the clams and heat through. Serve sprinkled with the fried garlic.

meat and poultry
carnes

I like this dish served on bread sautéed in good olive oil—
a bit rich, but very delicious. Try to find a smoked salted
bacon from Galicia called *panceta ahumada*; otherwise use
smoked slab bacon. Smoked paprika is easy to find now,
but unsmoked will be good too. In cooking, I use
manzanilla, a dry sherry named after the camomile herb;
it has a slightly bitter, astringent note like its namesake.

sautéed chicken livers
hígadillos salteados

3 tablespoons extra virgin olive oil

1 medium onion, finely chopped

2 garlic cloves, crushed

4 oz. chopped smoked Spanish panceta
or smoked slab bacon

4 sprigs of thyme

8 oz. chicken livers, trimmed and cut in half

¼ teaspoon smoked hot paprika (smoked
pimentón picante), plus extra for dusting

3 tablespoons manzanilla sherry

2 tablespoons chopped fresh flat-leaf parsley

sea salt and freshly ground black pepper

Fried bread

6 slices of white bread, crusts removed,
cut into triangles

extra virgin olive oil, for sautéing

Serves 4

To make the fried bread, heat the olive oil in a large skillet, add the triangles
of bread, and sauté on both sides until golden. Remove and drain on
paper towels.

Heat 2 tablespoons of the olive oil in a skillet, add the onion and garlic, and
sauté over low heat for 5 minutes until completely softened but not browned.

Increase the heat, add the panceta and thyme, and sauté for about
5 minutes until everything is golden. Transfer to a plate.

Wipe the pan with paper towels. Heat the remaining oil in the pan, then
add the chicken livers, paprika, salt, and pepper and sauté over high heat
until golden on both sides and soft in the middle (they will spit, so take care).

Transfer to the plate with the onion mixture. Deglaze the pan with the
manzanilla until almost evaporated, then return the contents of the plate
to the pan. Add the parsley, stir, and serve immediately on the fried bread.
Dust with a little extra paprika.

Huge quantities of garlic are essential and should be eaten squashed onto the chicken. My sister-in-law, a long-time Spanish resident, is addicted to this dish, judging by all the finger-licking and moans of approval, all spoken in her best Spanish. I have not quite mastered the accent, but I have managed to impress her with my recipe. Pollo al Ajillo is eaten with the fingers, and in restaurants is usually served with fries (page 99), so it is certainly a hands-on dish. Lots of paper napkins will be required—and a modern Penedès white wine made from unoaked Chardonnay would be a suitable companion.

chicken with garlic
pollo al ajillo

1 tablespoon sweet paprika (pimentón dulce)

1 tablespoon all-purpose flour

3½ lb. chicken pieces, such as thighs and breasts (but no drumsticks)

½ cup virgin olive oil

15 garlic cloves, unpeeled but bruised slightly

1 fresh bay leaf

½ cup medium dry sherry

1 tablespoon coarsely chopped fresh flat-leaf parsley

a heat-diffusing mat

Serves 4

Put the paprika, flour, salt, and pepper in a plastic bag and shake to mix. Add the chicken pieces and toss again until the chicken is evenly coated. Leave in the bag for 30 minutes or longer.

Heat the oil in a skillet, add the garlic, and sauté for 2 minutes, then remove with a slotted spoon. Add the chicken pieces (if necessary do half at a time, but remember to remove half the garlic-infused oil) and sauté for 5 minutes. Add the garlic and continue sautéing for 5 minutes until the chicken is golden on all sides.

Add the bay leaf and sherry and bring to a boil. Lower the heat and simmer gently on a heat-diffusing mat for about 30 minutes until tender. (The breast pieces will cook faster, so remove them about 10 minutes before the end of cooking.) Pile on a serving platter and sprinkle with parsley.

Note Although Pollo al Ajillo is traditionally cooked on top of the stove, it could be baked in a preheated oven at 375°F for 35 minutes or until cooked through.

Ask your butcher to prepare the pork loin ready for stuffing. To prepare it yourself, see the note below. Serve with a light, juicy red from Rioja.

stuffed pork loin
lomo de cerdo relleno

1 cup blanched almonds

3 tablespoons olive oil

1 medium onion, chopped

1 garlic clove, crushed

2 oz. cubed Spanish panceta or slab bacon

8 oz. salchicha sausages or any good spicy fresh pork sausage, skins removed*

1½ tablespoons finely chopped fresh flat-leaf parsley

2 lb. pork loin

1 cup dry white wine

coarse sea salt and freshly ground black pepper

Serves 4–6

Salchicha is a fresh pork sausage from Spanish stores. Botifarra blancas, a mild cured fresh sausage, is also good, as are Italian coarse pork sausages.

Put the almonds in a dry skillet and cook over gentle heat, shaking the pan, until lightly golden. Take care, because they burn easily. Tip onto a plate, let cool, then chop finely.

Heat 2 tablespoons of the oil in a skillet, add the onion and garlic, and sauté for about 5 minutes until softened but not browned. Transfer to a plate and let cool. Wipe out the pan, add the panceta, sauté without oil until golden, then add to the onions.

When the onion mixture is cool, put it in a bowl with the sausage meat, toasted almonds, and parsley, season with salt and pepper, and mix well.

Open out the pork, sprinkle with salt and pepper, cover, and set aside for 30 minutes.

Spread the stuffing all over the inside surface of the pork, leaving a 1-inch border all around. Roll up and tie with kitchen twine at 1-inch intervals. Season the outside with salt and pepper.

Heat the remaining oil in a heatproof casserole dish, add the pork, and sauté on all sides until golden. Add the wine and bring to a boil. Transfer the casserole dish to a preheated oven at 450°F and cook uncovered for 20 minutes. Reduce the heat to 350°F, cover the casserole dish, and cook for another 20 minutes for each 1 lb. in weight (40 minutes). Uncover for the last 10 minutes. Let the meat rest for 10–15 minutes, then slice thickly and serve.

Note To prepare the loin ready for stuffing, put the pork, flesh side down, on a cutting board—the loin should be at right angles to yourself. Using a long knife, make an incision about ¾ inch deep the length of the loin. Roll back the edge and continue cutting lengthways keeping a ¾ inch thickness. Follow the line of the circle, folding back the meat so it lies flat on the board. You will have a flat piece of meat, ready to spread with stuffing.

A robust country dish from Asturias in the cooler north of Spain, fabada consists of typical local ingredients; *fabes* (fat white beans), *lacón* (cured pork), panceta (cured bacon), morcilla (black pudding), and chorizo, all cooked in the same pot. It was typical winter peasant fare and has become a classic dish, appreciated all over the country. Serve it with cornbread and cider, specialities of Asturias, or with a classic Rioja.

beans with ham
fabada asturiana

2 cups fabes (large dried white beans), cannellini, or white haricot beans, covered with cold water and soaked overnight

2 bay leaves

a large pinch of saffron threads, toasted in a dry skillet and ground to a powder

1 onion, cut into fourths through the root

12 oz. piece of cured pork shoulder or lacón (Spanish cured pork), soaked overnight if salty

6 oz. morcilla or other black pudding (optional)

6 oz. sweet chorizo, or other chorizo suitable for cooking

1 tablespoon extra virgin olive oil

2 garlic cloves, crushed

1 tablespoon sweet paprika (pimentón dulce)

a heat-diffusing mat

Serves 4–6

Drain the beans and put in a saucepan with 6 cups cold water and the bay leaves. Bring to a boil for 5 minutes, then throw in 1 cup cold water to *asustar* or "scare" the beans. Immediately skim any froth off the surface and boil again for 5 minutes. Repeat the scare treatment and skim again.

Return to a boil for 5 minutes, add the saffron and onion, lower the heat to a simmer, and add all the meats. Simmer very gently using a heat-diffusing mat for about 2 hours until everything has cooked. Alternatively, bring to a boil on top of the stove, then cook in a preheated oven at 350°F for the same time.

During this time, keep the water level topped up to cover everything and occasionally skim and discard the red oil that rises to the surface.

When everything is soft, remove the meats, put in a deep serving dish and keep them warm. Put the beans in a bowl and keep them warm too.

Using a baster, remove 1 cup liquid from the pot, leaving any red oil behind. Heat the olive oil in a skillet, add the garlic and paprika, and sauté until crisp. Add the 1 cup liquid from the pot to deglaze the pan and pour into a blender with 3 tablespoons of cooked beans and the onion. Pulse to form a coarse purée, then stir into the bowl of beans.

Cut the meat into thick slices and return to the serving dish. Add the bean mixture and serve.

Spanish fries and pimientos de Padrón are the classic accompaniments for broiled meats. Spanish fries, served with almost every restaurant entrée in Spain, are the best I've ever tasted, and the secret is the excellent olive oil used for frying. Good companions would be a hearty Tempranillo or Garnacha-based red from Rioja or a rustic red from La Mancha such as Marqués de Griñon.

4 rib eye steaks, 1 inch thick

⅓ cup extra virgin olive oil

freshly squeezed juice of 1 lemon

3 garlic cloves, crushed

3 tablespoons finely chopped flat-leaf parsley

sea salt and freshly ground black pepper

Salsa de aceitunas

¼ cup olive oil

1 tablespoon sherry vinegar

4 oz. mixed pitted green and black olives

2 garlic cloves, crushed

2 firm tomatoes, peeled, seeded, and finely chopped

sea salt and freshly ground black pepper

To serve (optional)

pimientos de Padrón (page 16)

Spanish fries (see note)

Serves 4

pan-grilled steaks with olive sauce
entrecôte a la plancha con salsa de aceitunas

Put the steaks in a flat dish, sprinkle with the garlic, pepper, and half the parsley, pour over the oil and lemon juice, and rub in. Set aside for 2 hours or overnight in the refrigerator. Remove from the refrigerator 30 minutes before cooking and sprinkle with salt.

Meanwhile, to make the salsa, put the oil in a bowl and whisk in the sherry vinegar. Put the olives in a processor and blend to chop into small, evenly sized bits (not a purée). Put in the bowl with the oil mixture, add the rest of the ingredients, and season lightly.

When ready to cook the steak, heat a ridged stovetop grill-pan over high heat. When smoking, add the steaks and cook for 1½ minutes on each side for rare, 2 for medium, and 2½–3 for well done. Alternatively, cook on the outdoor grill. Sprinkle with the rest of the parsley and serve with the salsa and pimientos de Padrón and Spanish fries, if using.

Note To make Spanish fries, put 1½ lb. potatoes into ¼-inch slices, then into ¼-inch fingers. Rinse well in cold water to remove the starch, then pat dry on paper towels.

Fill a deep-fryer with pure olive oil to the manufacturer's recommended level and heat to 350°F. Working in batches, fry the potatoes until golden, then drain on paper towels and keep hot.

JUDIAS
DORADAS
kilo 4.50€

JUDIAS
CARITAS
kilo 3.40€

JUDIAS
MANTECA
kilo 3.31.

HIGOS
KILO 4.20€

PIÑONES
100 GRAMOS 3.00€

PASAS
-SIN HUESOS.-
KILO 6...€

UN-MANOJO
1.25 €

PIMIENTOS

0.49
EL 1⁄4

TOMATES
Kilo

UN-MANOJO
1 €

vegetables and legumes
verduras y legumbres secas

For this recipe, you need the tiny, often purplish green variety of artichoke, available in early summer before it develops the hairy choke above the heart. Jamón serrano or country ham is delicious and can be eaten as is, or cooked as in this recipe.

If you serve this dish as part of a tapas selection, try it with a crisp sherry with a tangy sea-fresh quality, such as a manzanilla from the seaside town of Sanlúcar de Barrameda.

artichokes with cured ham
alcachofas con jamón serrano

1½ lb. very small artichokes
1 lemon, halved
¼ cup extra virgin olive oil
8 slices jamón serrano or prosciutto, chopped
3 tablespoons chopped fresh flat-leaf parsley
sea salt and freshly ground black pepper

Serves 4

Fill a saucepan with water and squeeze in the lemon juice. Add the squeezed halves of lemon and some salt.

Trim the stalk of each artichoke to ½ inch, then trim off all the outer leaves until you reach the tender inner leaves. Cut the artichoke in half lengthwise. As you prepare them, add to the pan of lemon water to stop them turning brown.

Bring to a boil, then lower the heat and simmer for about 7 minutes until just tender. Drain and dry.

Heat the oil in a skillet, add the artichokes cut side down, and sauté for 5 minutes. Turn them over and sauté the other side for a further 2 minutes. Add the jamón serrano and sauté for a further 4 minutes until crisp and golden. Sprinkle with parsley and pepper and serve.

Note Spanish ham is of excellent quality. Jamón serrano is a delicious mountain ham, but the queen of hams is pata negra, from the handsome black Iberico pig. Pata negra is highly prized and expensive, so is used as a tapa in its own right, not for cooking.

Green beans are a great favorite in Spain. There are many recipes, but this is the one I like. If you add the dressing while the beans are still warm, they absorb more of the flavors. Delicious! I like this bean dish as a appetizer with a glass of fino, as well as an accompaniment to meat or fish.

2 large shallots
2 tablespoons white wine vinegar
1 garlic clove
a pinch of sugar
¼ cup extra virgin olive oil
1 lb. thin green beans
1 tablespoon chopped fresh flat-leaf parsley
1 hard-cooked egg, finely chopped
sea salt and freshly ground black pepper

Serves 6–8

green beans with dressing
judias verdes a la vinagreta

Put the chopped shallot in a small bowl and pour over 1 tablespoon of the vinegar and 1 tablespoon water.

Crush the garlic to a paste with the sugar and a pinch of salt. Add pepper and the remaining vinegar and gradually whisk in the oil to make a dressing.

Cook the beans in a saucepan of boiling salted water for about 4 minutes until just cooked but still crisp. Drain, transfer to a serving dish, pour over the dressing, and mix well. Rinse and drain the shallot. Sprinkle the shallot, egg, and parsley on top of the beans and serve warm or cold.

Variations
• Serve sprinkled with Migas (page 19) instead of hard-cooked egg.
• Instead of hard-cooked egg, add a fried egg to make a delicious light dish for lunch.
• Instead of beans, use thick white asparagus or regular green asparagus.
• Add canned red kidney beans or chickpeas, drained and rinsed well, then mixed through the green beans.

Note For a more contemporary approach to sherry drinking, serve fino well-chilled in normal wine glasses. At 15 percent alcohol, it is not very much stronger than a California Chardonnay, but drier and more tangy.

Every January, a uniquely Catalan festival, La Calçotada, celebrates the arrival of the *calçot* (pronounced "cal-shot") and spring. They are grilled over fires of vine cuttings until blackened and charred—eating them is a messy business and a real community affair. They are served wrapped in newspaper: this helps to complete the cooking and also steams off the charred outer layer so you can get to the sweet white flesh inside. This is a wonderful appetizer for a barbecue party—serve it with a bowl of the classic Salsa Romesco for dipping.

40 large scallions or salad onions, with large bulbous white sections

2 tablespoons olive oil

coarse sea salt

Salsa romesco

20 blanched almonds, toasted in a dry skillet

4 garlic cloves, unpeeled and blanched in cold water until soft, then peeled and chopped

2 dried chiles, such as romesco or ñora, soaked in boiling water for 20 minutes, then seeded and chopped, or 2 roasted red bell peppers from a jar

3 tomatoes, peeled, seeded, and chopped

2 teaspoons sweet paprika (pimentón dulce)

½ teaspoon chile flakes

½ cup red wine vinegar

1 cup olive oil

sea salt and finely ground black pepper

Serves 4

grilled scallion shoots with romesco sauce
calçots con salsa romesco

To make the salsa romesco, grind the almonds very finely in a coffee grinder. Put the ground almonds, garlic, peppers, tomatoes, paprika, chile flakes, and vinegar in a blender or food processor, then purée until smooth. Add salt and pepper, then drizzle in the oil gradually, with the motor running. Transfer to a small bowl.

Preheat a ridged stovetop grill-pan or outdoor grill. Toss the spring onions in olive oil and salt, then grill until blackened and charred on the outside. Remove from the pan, then wrap in newspaper for 25 minutes until softened further. Serve with the salsa romesco and finger bowls, napkins, and the traditional bibs if you want.

Notes Fatter, more bulbous scallions are often sold in supermarkets as "salad onions." Middle Eastern stores also stock very large varieties. Failing that, buy the largest scallions you can find and decrease the cooking time.

A clever Spanish housewife's trick for cooking dried beans is to *asustar* or "scare" the beans with cold water several times during cooking. This will stop the beans softening too quickly on the outside before they cook on the inside. It's also said to stop the beans splitting, but to achieve this, they must always be covered with liquid. I find it's also an effective way of quickly stopping them from boiling over—and also helps when you skim the froth so you don't remove the solids too. This recipe is found in the fishing villages of Asturias and Cantabria on the Bay of Biscay; for me it's comfort food, fit for kings.

white beans with clams
alubias blancas con almejas

1¼ cups Spanish dried white beans (alubias), white haricot beans, or cannellini beans, soaked for 24 hours or overnight

1 onion, halved

3 garlic cloves, peeled

1 carrot, halved

1 fresh bay leaf

a sprig of parsley

a small pinch of saffron, soaked in 1 tablespoon boiling water

salt

crusty bread, to serve

Clams

½ cup dry white wine

36 small clams

¼ cup olive oil

1 onion, finely chopped

2 garlic cloves, crushed

1 tablespoon sweet paprika (pimentón dulce)

1 medium dried red chile, such as guindilla or chipotle, seeded and coarsely ground

2 tablespoons coarsely chopped fresh flat-leaf parsley

sea salt and freshly ground black pepper

a medium-size piece of cheesecloth

Serves 4

Drain the soaked beans and put in a large saucepan with 1 quart cold water.

Add the onion halves, garlic, carrot, bay leaf, and parsley and bring slowly to a boil. When the froth threatens to boil over, splash 1 cup cold water into the pan to "scare" the beans. Skim off the froth, return to a boil, and simmer for 10 minutes. Splash another 1 cup cold water into the pan, return to simmering point, then continue cooking for about 1 hour until tender. Remove the onion, carrot, and parsley, add salt, and cook for another 5 minutes. Drain over a bowl, then put the beans back into the pan with the saffron, its soaking water, and ½ cup of the bean cooking liquid. Keep the lid on until ready to use. This stage can be done in advance.

To prepare the clams, heat the wine in a saucepan until boiling, add a little salt, then the clams. Cook, covered, for about 2 minutes until they open. (Discard any that don't.) Drain through a colander set over a bowl and cover with a plate. Rinse out the saucepan, add the oil, and heat for 30 seconds. Add the onions and garlic, cover, and cook over low heat for about 10 minutes without browning. Stir in the paprika and a little salt and pepper.

Remove half the clams from their shells and discard the shells. Add all the clams to the onions and carefully pour the clam liquid through a cheesecloth-lined strainer into the pan taking care to leave ½ inch in the bottom of the bowl because this may contain some grit. Heat the mixture just enough to warm up the clams.

Heat the beans and add the clam mixture. Ladle into heated soup plates. Sprinkle with parsley and serve with bread.

I use small brown lentils because they stay firm during cooking, but the big green ones called castellanas have a good flavor too. Lentil hotpots are the hearty comfort food of the Pyrenean valleys of Aragón, and they are also cooked with a ham bone to flavor them, then served with delicious Spanish morcilla (black pudding) and vegetables.

Suitable companions for this dish would be elegant reds made from blends of Cabernet Sauvignon and the local Tempranillo, such as Somontano, or softer reds based on Garnacha or easy-drinking Campode Borja.

1¼ cups small lentils, rinsed

3 tablespoons extra virgin olive oil

1 onion, finely chopped

1 garlic clove, crushed

2 tablespoons butter

4 oz. small cremini mushrooms

4 oz. oyster mushrooms, cut in half if large

3 tablespoons chopped fresh flat-leaf parsley

1 teaspoon freshly squeezed lemon juice

sea salt and freshly ground black pepper

To serve

6–12 slices bacon

leaves from a small bunch of flat-leaf parsley, half chopped, the rest left whole

Serves 6

sautéed lentils with mushrooms
lentejas salteadas con setas

Put the lentils in a saucepan, cover with 1 quart cold water, and bring to a boil. Lower the heat and simmer for about 35 minutes or until tender (the time will depend on the age of the lentils). Drain.

Heat 2 tablespoons of the oil in a skillet, add the onion and garlic, and sauté for about 10 minutes until soft and pale golden. Add the butter, the remaining oil, and the mushrooms. Stir-fry until the mushrooms are just cooked. Add the lentils, chopped parsley, lemon juice, salt, and pepper and continue to stir until heated through.

Meanwhile, broil the bacon until crisp. Serve the lentils topped with the parsley and 1–2 slices of bacon per serving.

Variations To make 2 other classic lentil dishes:
• Add 6 oz. cubed Spanish panceta instead of the mushrooms.
• Add 4 peeled, seeded, chopped tomatoes instead of the mushrooms.

Choose onions about the size of shallots, but not quite as small as pickling onions. A fast way to peel them and to keep a nice shape is to put them in a bowl or saucepan, cover with boiling water, drain, then rinse in cold water—the skins just fall off.

This is an excellent way to cook small onions. In Spain, large yellow onions are very sweet and are often eaten raw after being soaked in water for a little while—a habit that is said to go back to the Moors.

braised onions
cebollas guisadas

1½ lb. small onions

¼ cup olive oil

4 garlic cloves, peeled and halved lengthwise

a sprig of bay leaves

1 teaspoon smoked sweet paprika (smoked pimentón dulce)

¼ cup dry white wine

sea salt and freshly ground black pepper

Serves 4

Peel the onions, but leave the root end on.

Heat the oil in a heavy or cast-iron casserole dish with a lid. Add the onions, garlic, and bay leaves and cook over medium heat for 5 minutes. Stir often to stop them browning.

Add the paprika, salt, pepper, and wine, cover, and cook slowly until just tender, about 25 minutes (however, they can take up to 45 minutes depending on size).

Potatoes were introduced from the New World in the early 16th century, and now are more of a staple in the Spanish kitchen than almost any other ingredient. They are usually either fried in oil until crisp or cooked in stock, so this recipe is a combination of the two methods.

potatoes in shirts
patatas en camisa

1 lb. potatoes

a pinch of saffron threads

2 eggs

1 tablespoon milk

½ cup all-purpose flour, seasoned with salt and pepper

1 large onion, finely chopped

1 cup hot clear chicken stock

2 tablespoons chopped flat-leaf parsley

sea salt and freshly ground black pepper

pure olive oil, for deep-frying, plus 2 tablespoons for sautéing

an electric deep-fryer (optional)

Serves 4

Cut the potatoes into ½-inch slices and put in a bowl of cold water to stop them discoloring.

Using a mortar and pestle, crush the saffron with a little salt. Put in a bowl with the eggs, milk, salt, and pepper and whisk well.

Drain the potato slices, pat dry with paper towels, then dip them first in the seasoned flour, then in the egg mixture.

Fill a saucepan or deep-fryer one-third full with the oil, or to the manufacturer's recommended level. Heat to 350°F.

Fry the potatoes, a batch at a time, until golden—they don't have to cook through. Remove and drain on paper towels.

Meanwhile heat the 2 tablespoons oil in a skillet, add the onion, and sauté until soft and pale golden. Transfer to an ovenproof casserole dish. Add the potatoes to the casserole, season with salt and pepper, sprinkle with half the parsley, then add the hot stock. Grind some extra pepper over the top and bake uncovered in a preheated oven at 400°F until the potatoes are tender and the stock has been absorbed.

Sprinkle with the remaining parsley, then serve.

Pisto Manchego, from La Mancha in the heart of Spain, is probably based on an earlier Moorish eggplant dish. The original didn't include tomatoes or peppers, because these weren't introduced from the New World until the 16th century, after the expulsion of the Moors. This dish is very good eaten cold. However, I also like it served warm with a hot poached egg on top, or with a plate of Spanish Fries (page 99) or fried bread. Both accompaniments are particularly good when cooked in good Spanish olive oil.

vegetable sauté
pisto manchego

⅔ cup extra virgin olive oil

2 onions, chopped

4 garlic cloves, finely chopped

½ teaspoon cumin seeds

2 medium eggplant, chopped into ½-inch cubes

6 tomatoes, peeled, seeded, and chopped, with the juices reserved

10 oz. zucchini, cut into ½-inch cubes

3 large roasted red bell peppers from a jar, cut into ½-inch cubes

1 tablespoon coarsely chopped oregano, plus some leaves to serve

2 teaspoons sherry vinegar or red wine vinegar

sea salt and freshly ground black pepper

Serves 4–6

Heat half the oil in a heavy saucepan, add the onion and garlic, and sauté over medium heat for 5 minutes until softened. Remove to a bowl. Increase the heat, add the remaining oil, the cumin, and eggplant, stir until they take up the oil and soften slightly, then add the tomatoes and their juices. Simmer until the mixture starts to thicken.

Fold in the zucchini, peppers, and chopped oregano, season with salt and pepper, and simmer gently uncovered until soft. Fold in the vinegar and serve hot or cold with the oregano sprinkled over.

Note Traditional versions of this recipe often cook the vegetables to form a thick sauce, but I prefer them to keep their shape.

The first young vegetables of spring are the stars of this *menestra* (stew) from the Basque country in northwest Spain. Use tiny potatoes, thin beans, asparagus, peas, and little fava beans just large enough to swell their pods. If you grow your own garlic, include the young green shoots as well.

braised spring vegetables
menestra de verduras

24 tiny new potatoes

2 tablespoons olive oil

2 tablespoons salted butter

4 oz. baby onions, thinly sliced

2 garlic cloves, finely chopped

4 slices smoked fatty bacon, cut into small pieces

6 oz. thin green beans

8 oz. thin asparagus

1½ cups shelled fava beans (1 lb. before podding), or extra peas

1½ cups peas, fresh or frozen

sea salt

Serves 6

Put the potatoes in a pan of boiling salted water, cook until soft, then drain.

Meanwhile, heat the olive oil and half the butter in a saucepan, add the onions and garlic, cover, and cook until very soft but not browned. Add the bacon and cook for 4 minutes. Turn off the heat and leave covered. Add the potatoes as soon as they are ready.

Put the beans in a pan of salted boiling water and cook for 2 minutes. Add the asparagus and cook for 1 minute. Add the fava beans and cook for 1 minute. Add the peas and cook for 1 more minute. (If the skins on the fava beans are too thick, cook them separately and pop them out of their skins.) Drain in a colander and refresh immediately under cold running water. This will stop them cooking further.

Meanwhile, put the saucepan of potatoes over medium heat, add the remaining butter, the green vegetables, and 2 tablespoons water. Mix gently and warm through with the lid on for a minute or so, then serve.

sweet things

postres

The Moorish version of horchata was made with pine nuts, seeds, and chufas or tiger nuts (which aren't nuts, but a tuberous root) and used as a "pick-me-up." Almonds can also be used and, on baking hot days, the drink can be found freshly made in *horchaterias* and ice cream parlors, chilled and delicious. As early as the 16th century, snow was used to chill fruit drinks, so it was quite a labor-intensive luxury.

horchata
chilled almond drink

2 cups blanched almonds, coarsely chopped

3 tablespoons sugar

freshly squeezed juice of 1 lemon

extra crushed ice, to serve

ground cinnamon, for dusting

Serves 4

Put the almonds, sugar, and 1 cup water in a blender and grind as finely as possible. Pour into a pitcher or bowl and add 2¾ cups boiling water. Set aside to infuse for several hours until completely cold. Pour through a fine-mesh nylon strainer into a pitcher or bowl, pressing the liquid through with the back of a ladle. Stir in the lemon juice and pour into a freezerproof container.

Freeze for about 1 hour until crystals start to form. Stir well and serve in tall glasses with extra crushed ice if using and a dusting of cinnamon.

iced lemon crush
granizado de limón

coarsely grated zest and freshly squeezed juice of 8 unwaxed lemons

1 cup sugar

extra crushed ice (optional)

Serves 4

Put the lemon zest and sugar in a saucepan with 1 cup cold water and bring to a boil for 5 minutes. Strain into a bowl. Add 2 cups cold water and the lemon juice, pour into a freezerproof container, and freeze for about 1 hour until ice crystals have formed around the edge. Break up with a fork and serve. Add extra crushed ice, if using.

Variation Coffee Ice or *Granizado de Café*

Put 2½ cups good-quality ground coffee in a heatproof bowl or French press, add 1 quart boiling water, then stir in 1½ cups sugar and the peeled zest from 1 unwaxed lemon. Let cool completely.

Pour through a fine-meshed strainer or push the plunger of the French press, pour into a freezerproof container, and freeze and fork as in the previous recipe.

Fresh fruit is the favorite way to end a meal in Spain—either unadorned or with a little piece of cheese. However, these two desserts are simple and keep the freshness of the fruit intact. Oranges have been favorites in Spain since the Portuguese first introduced sweet ones from China, and bitter Sevilles, used for marmalade, were brought by Arab traders from India. Strawberries from the town of Aranjuez, south of Madrid, are of superb quality, and in summer a little 19th-century steam train brings them to the markets in the capital.

fresh orange juice with strawberries
zumo de naranja con fresas

4 Valencia or other sweet juicy oranges

1 lb. strawberries, cut in half if large

6 oz. wild strawberries (frais de bois), if available, or extra strawberries

6 white sugar cubes, coarsely crushed, or 3 tablespoons regular sugar

Serves 6

Squeeze the oranges and use some of the flesh that falls away as you juice, so it's nice and bitty.

Soak the strawberries in the orange juice in a serving bowl with a little of the sugar sprinkled over. Serve with the remaining sugar in a separate bowl.

spanish fruit salad
macedonia de frutas

mixed fresh fruit, cut into pieces

sweet sherry, to taste

Serves 6

Cut melons into pieces, fruits such as apricots and peaches into wedges, and grapes or strawberries in half. Sprinkle with enough sweet sherry to flavor and moisten. Set aside for 15 minutes at room temperature to macerate, then serve.

The fig tree is as ancient to the landscape of Spain as the olive tree and both thrive in the hot, dry climate. The earliest variety is small, plump, and black, fruiting in early summer, with other varieties continuing into late summer. Black figs have thick skins; green figs have thin skins. Whichever you choose for this dish, make sure they are fully ripe—squeeze them gently in the palm of your hand. When ripe, they should give slightly. A slightly split and dewy skin also denotes ripeness.

fig fritters
buñuelos de higos

1 cup all-purpose flour, plus a little for dusting

1 egg

2 egg whites

a scant 1 cup white wine

finely grated zest of 1 unwaxed lemon

3 tablespoons sugar, plus extra for dusting

8 figs with stalks

safflower oil, for deep–frying

an electric deep-fryer (optional)

Serves 4-8

Put the flour in a bowl, make a hollow in the center, and break in the egg. Add a little of the wine and gradually whisk in the flour from the edges so it doesn't go in all at once. Mix in the rest of the wine and lemon zest, cover with plastic wrap, and set aside for 1 hour.

Put the egg whites in a bowl and whisk until soft peaks form. Add the sugar a spoonful at a time, whisking to make a shiny meringue.

If the batter has thickened beyond thick cream stage, stir in a drop of water to loosen it a little. Fold in the meringue.

Fill a saucepan or deep-fryer one-third full with the oil, or to the manufacturer's recommended level. Heat the oil to 375°F.

Dust the figs with a little flour and dip them in the batter. Add the figs to the hot oil, in batches if necessary. When the batter turns crisp and golden, remove with a slotted spoon, and drain on paper towels. Dust with sugar and serve while hot.

This classic Catalan dish has become famous all over Spain. It is similar to the French crème brûlée, but in Spain cornstarch is usually added. It is served in small cazuelas designed to be filled right to the top so the surface can be burnt with a branding iron (*quemadoro*) that has been heated over a gas flame until smoking hot. This instantly caramelizes the sugared surface. In the absence of this handy tool, use a blowtorch—household broilers aren't usually hot enough. If you visit Spain, a *quemadoro* makes an interesting gift for friends who love cooking.

catalan caramel cream
crema catalana

1 cup sugar

4 teaspoons cornstarch

6 extra-large egg yolks

2¾ cups heavy cream

1¾ cups whole milk

freshly grated zest from 1 unwaxed lemon

½ cinnamon stick

6 shallow cazuelas or ramekins, about 4¼ inches diameter x 1 inch deep

a cook's blowtorch

Serves 6

Mix ¾ cup of the sugar and the cornstarch in a bowl. Stir in the egg yolks until smooth, but do not whisk or the mixture will form a froth.

Put the cream, milk, lemon zest, and cinnamon in a saucepan and heat gently until it just reaches boiling point. Pour onto the egg yolk mixture and stir well. Rinse out the pan and add the mixture. Stir over a low heat with a wooden spoon until it thickens enough to coat the spoon. Remove from the heat, leave to infuse for 30 minutes, then strain into a pitcher. Pour into the 6 dishes and chill for about 12 hours.

Sprinkle over the remaining sugar and caramelize the sugar with a blowtorch. As the caramel cools, it will harden. The dishes can be left for up to 1 hour, but don't put them in the refrigerator or the caramel may soften if left too long.

Note Traditional mini-cazuelas are made of terra cotta, and widely available in kitchen stores and by mail order (page 142).

A more delicious version of French toast, *torrija* is one of Spain's best-loved treats. It is a sweet bread fritter that is eaten for dessert or in *confiserías* (cake shops) as a snack with a *café cortado* (coffee with a "cut" of milk). Easter is the big time for torrijas, but you find them all year round. In Spain, you would use the everyday *pan de pueblo*—a long loaf with a crisp crust. At home, I use a baguette.

cinnamon toast with honey
torrijas con canela y miel

⅔ cup milk

1 vanilla bean, split lengthwise

freshly grated zest of 1 unwaxed lemon

3 eggs, beat

1 long baguette-style loaf, cut into 8 slices

¼ cup moscatel wine

olive oil, for cooking

To serve

⅓ cup honey

ground cinnamon, for dusting

5 sugar cubes, coarsely crushed, or 2½ tablespoons regular sugar

Serves 4–8

Put the milk in a saucepan with the vanilla bean and lemon zest and heat to just below boiling point. Remove from the heat and let cool. When cool, beat in the eggs.

Strain the mixture into a flat dish large enough to take 2 slices of bread at a time. Put the slices of bread on a tray and sprinkle with the wine, just to moisten slightly.

Dip 2 slices of bread into the egg mixture and let soak for a few minutes. Heat the oil in a skillet over medium heat, add the soaked bread, and sauté until golden brown on both sides, about 4 minutes. Drain on paper towels. Repeat until all are done.

Transfer to a large serving dish and spoon over the honey, sprinkle with cinnamon and sugar, and either let soak for a few hours or eat while hot.

If eating them cold, add the sugar just before serving.

Named after the patron saint of Spain, this cake is common in Galicia, where there is a shrine to St. James (Iago) in Santiago de Compostella. It is traditionally adorned with a stencil pattern of his sword using confectioners' sugar. It is a flourless, butterless cake with whole almonds still in their skins, finely ground. You must use a coffee grinder or spice grinder—an ordinary food processor will not grind them finely enough. Alternatively, you can use ordinary ground almonds, but the flavor and color will be different.

st. james's cake
tarta de santiago

1¾ cups (8 oz.) whole almonds, with skins
6 extra-large eggs, separated
1 cup sugar
a large pinch of ground cinnamon
confectioners' sugar, for dusting
butter, for greasing
fine sea salt

*a deep springform cake pan
10 inches diameter,
greased with butter and base-lined
(slash the paper so it reaches
1 inch up the sides)*

Serves 8–12

Using a clean coffee grinder, grind the almonds until fine, with no lumps.

Put the egg whites and a pinch of salt in a bowl and whisk until soft peaks form. Whisk in half the sugar, 1 tablespoon at a time, to stabilize the whites.

Whisk the yolks with the remaining sugar and cinnamon until thick and the volume has increased. The mixture should leave a trail when you raise the whisk from the bowl.

Fold the ground almonds into the egg yolk mixture. Fold in a little of the whites to loosen the mixture, then fold in the remainder. Spoon into the pan and bake in a preheated oven at 350°F for about 45 minutes until cooked, golden and firm but springy. Check after 35 minutes—if it is over-browning, cover with wax paper and continue baking.

Remove from the oven and let cool in the pan on a wire rack for 10 minutes, then invert onto the rack to cool completely. Dust with confectioners' sugar using a stencil of St. James's sword if you wish.

Soplillos Granadinos were popular in Granada, the last stronghold of the Moors, who ruled Spain for 800 years until expelled by the Inquisition in the late 15th century. During that time, they influenced Spanish kitchens to a huge extent, not least by introducing almonds to the repertoire of ingredients. Interestingly, Christian nuns took over the confectionery business when the Moors left Granada.

Serve with a bowl of whipped cream, *nata montada*, for dipping, and a *café cortado*—coffee with just a "cut" of milk.

moorish almond meringues
soplillos granadinos

3 egg whites

a pinch of sea salt

1 cup sugar

finely grated zest of 1 unwaxed lemon

½ teaspoon pure vanilla bean paste (see note) or the scraped-out seeds of 1 vanilla bean

½ cup toasted almond flakes, chopped into small pieces

whipped cream, to serve

a pastry bag, fitted with a 1-inch plain tip

mini muffin papers (optional)

2 nonstick baking sheets

Makes about 36

Put the egg whites in a bowl with a pinch of salt and whisk until just firm. Add the sugar, 2 tablespoons at a time, whisking after each addition. Carefully fold in the zest, vanilla, and almonds so as not to lose volume.

Fill the pastry bag with the mixture. Pipe the meringue either into double mini muffin papers set on the baking sheets or straight onto the baking trays. Bake in a preheated oven at 250°F for 30 minutes.

Increase the heat to 275°F for a further 20 minutes. Remove from the oven, let cool on a wire rack, and serve in their cases with a bowl of whipped cream. (Remove the outer muffin case before serving.)

Variation This mixture can be made into cookies or *almendrados*. Double the amount of almonds, and grind them to a fine powder in a spice grinder or coffee mill. Drop heaping teaspoons onto greased baking trays and cook in a preheated oven at 275°F for 15 minutes. They will be soft when they come out of the oven, but firm up when cold.

Note Vanilla paste is found in larger supermarkets, often in the gourmet food department. For mail order suppliers, see page 142. If you can't find it, use the seeds from 1 vanilla bean.

After a night of revelry doing what Spaniards do best (eating, drinking, and talking), churros and hot chocolate at dawn is compulsory, ensuring a blissful sleep. The basic mixture is a flour and water dough, but I prefer this variation with egg and lemon zest, which makes the dough softer and easier to push through a piping bag. A churros maker or *churrera* is a perfect souvenir for the keen cook to take home from Spain. Inexpensive and very efficient, it is a fat plastic tube with a screw-down plunger and ridged tip.

A *chocolate a la taza* (cup of hot chocolate) for dunking churros must be thick—more like a sauce than a drink. The commercial chocolate made for the purpose has rice flour in it, which I prefer instead of the cornstarch thickener used when people make churros at home.

churros with hot chocolate
churros con chocolate a la taza

a pinch of salt

finely grated rind of 1 unwaxed lemon

1 teaspoon safflower oil, plus extra for deep-frying

1 cup all-purpose flour, sifted

1 egg, beaten with 1 tablespoon cold water

sugar, for dusting

Chocolate a la taza

8 oz. semisweet chocolate, about 50 percent cocoa solids, broken into squares

2 tablespoons sugar

a stick of cinnamon

2 tablespoons fine rice flour

an electric deep-fryer (optional)

a strong pastry bag fitted with a star tip, or a Spanish churros maker

a wide oiled spatula

Makes about 12: serves 4

To make the churros, put 1 cup cold water in a medium saucepan with the salt, lemon zest, and 1 teaspoon oil. Bring to a fast boil, then add the flour all at once. Beat quickly with a wooden spoon to bring the mixture to a smooth paste, then leave for 5 minutes. Beat the egg mixture into the paste a little at a time until smooth and thick.

Fill a saucepan or deep-fryer one-third full with the oil, or to the manufacturer's recommended level. Heat to 375°F.

Working in batches if necessary, spoon the mixture into the pastry bag. Pipe horseshoe shapes onto the oiled spatula, cutting the flow of dough at 6-inch intervals with a knife or scissors. Slide them into the oil and fry for about 4 minutes until a rich gold, drain on paper towels, and dust with sugar, heaping it on top as well, in true Spanish style.

To make the Chocolate a la Taza, put the chocolate, sugar, and 3⅔ cups cold water in a saucepan with the cinnamon stick and slowly melt the chocolate. Put the rice flour in small bowl, add ¼ cup cold water and mix until smooth. Blend it into the chocolate, mix well, and bring just to a boil. If too thick, add a little water and reheat. Serve hot with the churros.

mail order addresses and websites

Authentic Spanish ingredients are just beginning to make their way onto the shelves of gourmet stores and quality supermarkets.

SPANISH FOOD AND UTENSILS

Amigofoods.com
Miami, FL 33138
Tel: 800 627 2544
www.store.amigofoods.com
A wide choice of foods from Spain, Central, and South America.

Buyspain.com
3130 Plaza Street
Las Vegas, NV 89121
Tel: 702 737 3925
Fax: 702 732 1033
www.buyspain.com
Imported Spanish utensils and products including paella pans, gas burners and tripods, paella spoons, cazuelas, and saffron.

www.chefshop.com
PO Box 3488
Seattle, WA 98114
Tel: 877 337 2491
Features a wide range of quality raw ingredients, plus condiments and seasonings. Oils, vinegars, beans, lentils, vanilla paste.

La Española Meats, Inc.
25020 Doble Avenue
Harbor City, CA 90710
Tel: 310 539 0455
Fax: 310 539 5989
Mon–Fri: 8:30–5 Sat–Sun: 9–5
www.laespanolameats.com
Spanish wines and sherries, foods such as,salt cod, membrillo, beans. Paella pans, terra cotta dishes.

GourmetSleuth.com
PO Box 508
Los Gatos, CA 95031
Tel: 408 354 8281
Fax: 408 395 8279
www.gourmetsleuth.com
Sherry vinegars, heat diffusers, blow torches.

www.ingredientsgourmet.com
Tel: 646 250 8394
An easy-to-navigate site featuring products from all around the Mediterranean. Spanish specialties include Manchego and Cabrales cheese, jamón serrano, chorizos, membrillo, arbequina olives, lentils, piquillo peppers, sherry vinegar, pimentones.

www.nielsenmassey.com.
Online source of vanilla paste.

www.penzeys.com
Tel: 800 741 7787
Herbs, spices, and seasonings, including white, green, or pink peppercorns and premium saffron. Shop online, request a catalog, or explore any one of 16 Penzeys Spice shops nationwide.

Shop Spain
110 Vista Center Drive
Forest, VA 24551
Tel: Toll Free 877 885 0660
Mon–Fri: 9–5 (ET)
www.shopspain.com
Hams, cheeses, beans, olives, wines, and sherries. Cookware, paella pans, ham holders, and utensils.

The Spanish Table
•1427 Western Ave
Seattle, WA 98101
Tel: 206 682 2827
Mon–Sat: 9:30–6, Sun: 11–5
•1814 San Pablo Ave
Berkeley, CA 94702
Tel: 510 548 1383
Mon–Sat: 10–6, Sun: 11–5
•109 North Guadalupe Street
Santa Fe, NM 87501
Tel: 505 986 0243
Mon–Sat: 10–6, Sun: 11–5
www.spanishtable.com
Olive oil, olives, Spanish rice, peppers and paprika, saffron, beans and lentils, cheeses, sausages, and ham. Wines including sherries, rosados, white wines, and cavas. Paella pans, cazuelas.

Tienda.com
Tel: 757 566 8606 / 888 472 1022
3701 Rochambeau Road
Williamsburg, VA 23188
www.tienda.com
This well-organized, easy-to-navigate website offers a treasure of Spanish speciality food products including cheese, Calasparra rice for paella, sweet, bittersweet or hot smoked paprika, pequillo peppers, aged sherry vinegars, and olive oil. Meats include jamón serrano (sliced or an entire ham) and many chorizos. Seafood offerings include salt cod. Cazuelas in various sizes, and a churros maker.

Zingermans
620 Phoenix Drive
Ann Arbor, Michigan 48108
422 Detroit Street
Ann Arbor, Michigan 48104
Tel: 888 636 8162 / 734 663 DELI
www.zingermans.com
Zingerman's selection of cheeses, estate-bottled olive oils and varietal vinegars is unmatched. Their website and catalog are packed with information. Spanish paprika and chorizo, cheese, vinegar, bomba rice, Spanish drinking chocolate.

SPANISH WINES

www.reservaycata.com
An interesting Madrid-based website describing Spanish wines and grape varieties.

Best Cellars Inc.
180 Varick Street
Fourth Floor
New York, NY 10014
Tel: 800 624 6250
212 989 2540 / 212 989 8530
www.bestcellars.com
Wine Online. Includes an excellent selection of Spanish wines. Has stores in Boston, Washington DC, Dallas, Houston, Oakton, Arlington, New York, and Great Barrington MA.

Zachys Wine
16 East Parkway
Scarsdale, NY 10583
Tel: 800 723 0241
Mon–Sat: 8–8
www.zachys.com
For wines from around the world, including a fine selection of Spanish wines.

GROW YOUR OWN

Chile Plants
PO Box 170
199 Kingwood-Locktown Road
Rosemont, NJ 08556-0170
Tel: 908 996 4646
Fax: 908 996 4638
www.chileplants.com
Said to be one of the world's largest suppliers of live chile plants. Includes a directory of chiles, bell peppers, and tomatoes.

index

conversion charts

Weights and measures have been rounded
up or down slightly to make measuring
easier.

Volume equivalents:

American	Metric	Imperial
1 teaspoon	5 ml	
1 tablespoon	15 ml	
¼ cup	60 ml	2 fl.oz.
⅓ cup	75 ml	2½ fl.oz.
½ cup	125 ml	4 fl.oz.
⅔ cup	150 ml	5 fl.oz. (¼ pint)
¾ cup	175 ml	6 fl.oz.
1 cup	250 ml	8 fl.oz.

Weight equivalents: **Measurements:**

Imperial	Metric	Inches	Cm
1 oz.	25 g	¼ inch	5 mm
2 oz.	50 g	½ inch	1 cm
3 oz.	75 g	¾ inch	1.5 cm
4 oz.	125 g	1 inch	2.5 cm
5 oz.	150 g	2 inches	5 cm
6 oz.	175 g	3 inches	7 cm
7 oz.	200 g	4 inches	10 cm
8 oz. (½ lb.)	250 g	5 inches	12 cm
9 oz.	275 g	6 inches	15 cm
10 oz.	300 g	7 inches	18 cm
11 oz.	325 g	8 inches	20 cm
12 oz.	375 g	9 inches	23 cm
13 oz.	400 g	10 inches	25 cm
14 oz.	425 g	11 inches	28 cm
15 oz.	475 g	12 inches	30 cm
16 oz. (1 lb.)	500 g		
2 lb.	1 kg		

Oven temperatures:

110°C	(225°F)	Gas ¼
120°C	(250°F)	Gas ½
140°C	(275°F)	Gas 1
150°C	(300°F)	Gas 2
160°C	(325°F)	Gas 3
180°C	(350°F)	Gas 4
190°C	(375°F)	Gas 5
200°C	(400°F)	Gas 6
220°C	(425°F)	Gas 7
230°C	(450°F)	Gas 8
240°C	(475°F)	Gas 9